GW00372146

Nuts

*Questo libro è dedicato ai fratelli Riccardo e Lucia Damiano che,
nel mese di febbraio 2004 in Sicilia, mi hanno regalato indimenticabili
fragranze di fiori di mandorli, alberi di pistacchi e boschi di noccioli ...*

*This book is dedicated to the brother and sister Riccardo and Lucia Damiano
who, in February 2004 in Sicily, offered me the unforgettable scents
of almond trees, pistachio trees and hazel trees.*

Maria Fredin Skoog

Nuts

100 recipes for nutritious nuts

Photography by Gunnar Nydrén

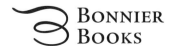

BONNIER BOOKS

Contents

IS IT POSSIBLE THAT there's any sector there isn't a cookery book about?
Yes. We've found it – it's all about nuts.

In an era when food and drink are becoming increasingly sophisticated and
when it's part of a rounded education to know the difference between different
cocoa beans in South America, we have found a gap. A gap we want to fill with
nuts and almonds! What do we actually know about the world's oldest food?
That little nutritional power pack which has helped keep the world's population
alive since the dawn of time and which tastes so good. And just think of all
the delicious things you can do with nuts! Take the aromatic Sicilian almond
for instance. When the almond trees bloom in February in the Valle dei Templi,
a creamy white sea unfurls and in the midst of it a few reddish-pink blossoms
– the flowers of the bitter almond. Like a symbol of love, which can be so
sweet and wonderful, but also terribly bitter.

Or take the delicious little hazelnuts which grow wild here, there and

everywhere in Northern Europe and the exquisite walnuts from Périgord in France or the alluring macadamia nuts from Queensland in Australia. In short there is so much to say and there are so many recipes to share involving nuts and almonds. Take for example our own domestic nut, the hazelnut. The little, silky, smooth, brown, shell and the little cap the hazelnut sits in, make it a pretty woodland jewel. Crack the shell and out comes a perfectly formed reddish-brown, little onion-shaped nut which is a vanilla-yellow colour beneath its thin outer skin – the kernel itself. Put it in your mouth, listen to the soft cracking noise when the kernel snaps and feel the sweet, rounded taste with a hint of bitterness and smooth oil. The hazelnut leaves behind a touch of astringency and yet moreishness in the mouth. It's difficult to stop cracking hazelnuts once you've started.

Welcome to the world of nuts!

Maria Fredin Skoog

Nuts, almonds and seeds

CASHEW NUTS

Anacardium occidentale, which belongs to the
Anacardiaceae (sumach) family, originally
came from the West Indies but is grown as a
fruit tree throughout the tropics. It was
probably the Portuguese who discovered
the cashew tree in Brazil in the sixteenth
century. Today the tree is particularly
common in southeast Asia and east Africa.

The plant is a tree about 15 metres tall.
After it has flowered the fruit stem swells
and forms what is called the cashew apple.
The kidney-shaped nut hangs directly from the
fruit, which is a false fruit but often seen as the actual
fruit. It looks rather strange, a bit like a yellow or red hat with a
knob on! Cashew nuts contain a seed, but are surrounded by a shell
containing an oil which is highly irritating to the skin. Therefore the nuts
are normally roasted so that the oil disappears before you can get to the
kernel. The cashew fruit is also edible and tastes a bit like an apple; you
can also make juice from it or dry the flesh. The fleshy leaves are also
used in cooking. Cashew nuts are always sold without their shells.
We import cashew nuts from South America and the USA.

*Store cashew nuts in a cool place, between 8-12°C, to keep them
at their best.*

HAZELNUTS

The hazel tree, *Corylus avellana,* which belongs to the Corylaceae family (hazel), originally came from southern Europe and the Middle East, which are still the main growing areas. The hazel tree is known throughout Europe

and on all the continents but it is grown very little outside Europe and the Middle East. Turkey is the biggest producing country. The shape and colour of the leaves vary a great deal from one variety to another. The trees flower before the leaves open. The male flowers form long catkins whilst the female flowers grow in clusters of two or three.

The fruit nestles in a calyx which almost surrounds the nut. The nut comprises a thick shell with a fatty embryo, surrounded by two cotyledons, which constitute the nut kernel and that is the part we use.

The fact that for many thousands of years people have sat and cracked hazelnuts and enjoyed the same great flavour engenders confidence in this plant. That of course was long before nutcrackers made life easier for people with a passion for nuts. Hazels grow both wild and in several cultivated forms in large parts of Europe, western Asia, North Africa and North America. 500,000 tonnes of nuts are produced each year, with the USA and Austria as the biggest exporters. But we import a lot of hazelnuts from Turkey and Italy, even though hazel trees grow naturally in the northern parts of Europe.

Hazel usually grows to about four metres but there are tree-like bushes which can grow up to almost twelve metres.

PEANUTS

Arachis hypogaea belongs to the Fabaceae (legume) family and is actually not a nut but a leguminous plant. It originally came from the tropical parts of South America, but it is chiefly grown in India, East and West Africa, China, Indonesia and southern USA. After America was discovered, the trading ships took peanuts to Africa. The Spaniards in their turn took the peanut to the Philippines and at the beginning of the twentieth century it came to India and China and at about the same time to the USA. It is now grown in all tropical and subtropical areas. India and China are the biggest producers.

The peanut plant is an annual with a tap root about 30 cm long. The yellow flowers are self-pollinating. The stalks of the flowers bend downwards and the fruits bury themselves about eight centimetres in the earth. Here the fruit, which is a pod with little encapsulated seeds, ripens. Think what a peanut looks like in its shell, the pod is easy to break open and the nuts have a thin reddish-brown skin. Peanuts which have not been roasted can be eaten directly from the pod and have a pleasant mild flavour.

Peanuts are best stored at -3°C, at which temperature they can keep for up to a year, otherwise as cool as possible in the refrigerator.
Room temperature is not recommended.

COCONUT

Cocos nucifera of the Arecaceae (palm) family belongs to the group of 'nuts' which are not really nuts! The coconut is a drupe and it can weigh up to three kilos. The shell is outermost, green and leathery. Under the shell is the fruit flesh, which is brown and full of masses of fibres. Inside sits the stone which is the part we call the coconut and the white flesh is the seed albumen which is eaten fresh, like the opaque liquid (which is incorrectly called coconut milk) which can be drunk directly from the fruit.

It is hard to imagine a more useful tree. The nuts can be eaten, the shells becomes bowls to eat out of or fuel to cook food over, the fibres can be used for cloth and rope and the trunk is timber. The coconuts and the tree can also be used for cosmetics, medicinal products and a number of chemical substances. The coconut palm was already to be found all over the tropical areas of Asia and Polynesia and along the Pacific coast of South America before America was discovered. It is impossible to say exactly where the coconut palm came from. The name itself created some confusion with cocoa initially. In London, when coconuts started to be imported into Europe, they are reported to have called them 'coker-nuts' for that reason.

The palm grows to about 30 metres and has a large fan-shaped crown of strong, five-metre-long laciniate leaves. Think of the sound of rustling palm trees and the surf breaking on a sun-drenched beach – then you are almost in paradise! The trunk is not more than 25 cm thick, but it is held in place by an impressive rootball comprising masses of strong roots which extend about five metres from the trunk.

We import coconuts all year round, chiefly from Central America

Coconuts should be stored in the refrigerator.

MACADAMIA NUTS

Macadamia integrifolia belongs to the Proteacean family and was discovered quite late by the western world. But for the aborigines in Australia, the macadamia nut has always been an important part of their diet.

For millennia, these nuts were highly prized by the aborigines, who can recount legends about the history of this nut. When the Europeans began to settle in Australia they exchanged tobacco and rum for the nuts. Since the nuts occurred mainly in Queensland, initially they were called Queensland nuts. But one of Australia's botanists, Ferdinand von Mueller, decided to give the nuts the name *macadamia* after his Scottish colleague, Dr. John McAdam, who died in 1865 after an adventurous journey from Australia to New Zealand.

The macadamia nut is the only native crop in Australia which has developed to be commercially grown. It is now also grown on Hawaii but the nuts from Queensland are still considered the best.

The nut grows on an evergreen tree with leathery leaves which can become up to 20 metres tall. The nut is surrounded by a thick green sheath, when the nut is ripe it falls to the ground and the sheath opens to reveal the nut. The nut is very hard to crack. After the nuts have been harvested they are dried for 14 days, after which they are cracked and sorted according to quality. The nut does not contain any cholesterol and in a study at the University of Queensland, it was claimed that eating macadamia nuts can even lower cholesterol levels in the blood. A cooking oil can also be made from the nuts, with a pleasant taste and good characteristics.

The nuts are on sale all the year round. They should be stored in the refrigerator or cooler, like other oleaginous nuts.

ALMONDS

Prunus amygdalus of the Rosaceae (rose) family, is not a nut, but a drupe and it is related to the cherry, peach and plum and is thought to have come originally from the western parts of Asia, Afghanistan and Iran, where the tree still grows wild. From there the almond tree spread across Europe, where it is cultivated, far up into Central Europe. California in the USA, Spain and Italy are among the main producer countries.

The almond tree is quite a small tree with slender branches. It flowers abundantly on bare twigs. Anyone who has been, for example, in Agrigento on the south coast of Sicily when the almond trees are in flower, knows what a beautiful sight it is. A billowing sea of white flowers, with here and there a touch of red. The red flowers turn into the bitter almonds and the redder the flower the more bitter the almond. They flower on the same tree as the sweet almonds. The fruit is grey-green, flat and covered with a velvety sheath.

There are different kinds of almond: the dessert almond is usually sold at Christmas, with a soft shell which you can almost crack with your fingers.

Sweet almonds are the ones we used for cooking, for baking, in desserts and in sweets.

Bitter almonds contain amygdalin. This is a glycoside which is converted among other things into toxic prussic acid when the almonds are chewed. Bitter almonds are often smaller and darker than sweet almonds.

Almonds should be stored in the refrigerator or the freezer.

BRAZIL NUTS

Bertholletia excelsa belongs to the Lecythidcaceae (Brazil nut) family and is actually not a nut, but a capsule fruit. The Brazil nut tree is enormous and can grow up to 50 metres tall. The capsule which contains the nuts, is reminiscent of a coconut and can weigh two kilos or more. The thick woody capsule can contain up to 25 nuts which grow like the segments of a citrus fruit. If you look at the nut with its shell on, you can clearly see the shape of a segment. There are almost no cultivated trees, but the Brazil nut tree grows wild in the Brazilian rainforests along the Amazon river. When the fruit is ripe it falls to the ground. It is probably highly dangerous to be underneath when these heavy capsules fall from a great height! The name 'Para', given to the nuts in some languages, comes from the area of Pará around the Amazon estuary where there is a port for shipping Brazil nuts. The Brazilians call the nut *castanheiro* meaning chestnut, but in the English-speaking part of the world they are called Brazil nuts.

Brazil nuts are in the shops all the year round. It's a good idea to store them in the freezer or the refrigerator. If properly stored the nuts can keep for up to a year.

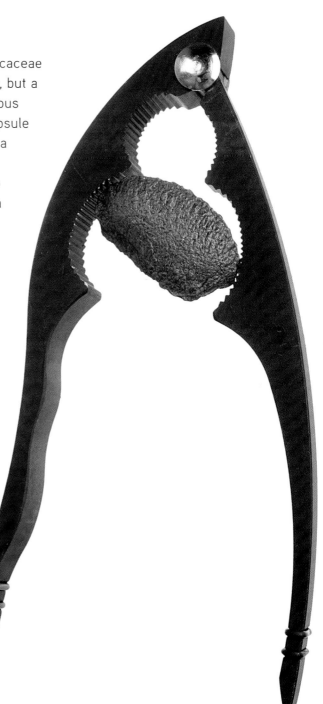

PECAN NUTS

Carya illininensis of the Juglandaceae (walnut) family was for many thousands of years as important a source of food for the North American Indians as the Macadamia nut was for the aborigines in Australia. The Pecan nut is believed to have the same capacity to lower blood cholesterol as the Macadamia nut. The nut is sometimes called the sweet little sister of the walnut. The two trees are related, but the Pecan nut has not yet become as common in Europe as the walnut. The tree still grows wild in North America but the biggest plantations in the USA are found in Texas. The tree is quite tall and needs a mild climate. The fruit consists of a fleshy outer layer. As distinct from the walnut the shell is smooth and shiny with a reddish brown colour. The nut is elongated and dark brown in colour and furrowed like a walnut..

Pecan nuts are grown in the USA, Mexico, China, Australia, South Africa, Israel and India.

Store them cool, preferably in the refrigerator. Nuts with the shell on can be stored for up to a year in the freezer.

PINE NUTS

Pinus pinea belongs to the Pinaceae (pine) family. Surely many of us have travelled in the countries around the Mediterranean and brought home huge pine cones? But it is only in recent years that pesto and pine nuts have made such an impact on our tables and we have understood the connection between the cones and the nuts. And like so many other cases where we talk about nuts, pine nuts are not nuts! In this case they are seeds. The cones are harvested between October and March and they are knocked down with very long sticks. So if you are thinking of standing under a pine tree at harvest time, it's a good idea to have something to protect your head! When the pine cone dries out and opens its scales, the pine seeds fall out. They are often in pairs under the scales. The same thing happens with our native pine cones, which are considerably smaller and it is the seeds inside the cones which the squirrels seek. The little elongated 'nuts' usually come from southern European pines whilst the small droplet-shaped 'nuts' are of Chinese origin.

A pine tree can grow to about 30 metres tall, live to be several hundred years old and it originates from the Mediterranean area. The cones only develop when the tree is about 25 years old. The crown of the tree is shaped like an umbrella and can be very broad and the trunk is often quite thick. The needles are long and grow in pairs. The cones are as big as a clenched fist. Pine trees are cultivated in Spain, Portugal and Italy. In the middle of June there is a pine festival in Chiesanuova, just outside Florence, the 'Sagra del Pinolo'. But the tree grows, and the nuts are used, throughout the world.

Store pine nuts like other nuts, between cool and cold, preferably in the refrigerator.

PISTACHIO NUTS

Pistacia vera belongs to the Anacardiaceae (sumach) family.

On the slopes of Mount Etna on Sicily, pistachio trees stand in the black lava looking like gnarled, greyish-white, dead trees during the winter months. Every other year the trees flower extra prolifically in April, particularly if there has been a cold winter, and it is an incomparably beautiful sight. The pistachio tree originally comes from western Asia and it is supposed to have been the Romans who brought it back with them to Europe. Since then it has been grown in the Mediterranean countries for a very long time and from there it has spread across Europe and America. Today it is mostly grown in Iran and in the USA.

The pistachio tree grows not more than two metres tall and can produce 20 kilos of nuts. The pinkish-white flowers, which may also be tinged with green and turquoise, are pollinated with the help of the wind. One in eight trees is usually a male plant. The fruit is a drupe with thin, slightly crinkled, leathery flesh. It surrounds a woody white stone which is what we call the pistachio nut. The nut consists of a little, angular, oval seed surrounded by a reddish-violet skin. It is this seed which we eat and its colour can range from yellowish-green to acid green and dark green. The greener the nuts the finer and more expensive they are. When the fruit is ripe the shell splits open at one end, it looks as if the nut is laughing. In Iran this stage is called 'khandan' which quite simply means 'laugh'. Pistachio nuts are Iran's third largest export product.

Pistachio nuts are available all the year round.

Pistachio nuts should be stored cold, at just a few degrees above zero, but they are best if stored at -3°C. Just like other nuts, it is best to keep them in the refrigerator if your freezer is not at -3°C.

WALNUTS

Juglans regia, the walnut, of the Juglandaceae (walnut) family, is a cultivated tree with a long history. It probably originated from the Balkan peninsula and the Middle East. Walnut trees are often planted as individual specimens, popularly as a 'sentinel tree'. As a lone tree it may grow up to 15 metres tall and have a wide spread. The leaves have a strong aroma and are large, comprising five to nine smaller, shiny leaves. The female flowers look like red stars, growing in groups of three and the male flowers are greenish-yellow catkins. The fruits are green. There is a fleshy layer on the outside, which splits open when the nut ripens and comes off.

The walnut may be susceptible to frost. But in Northern Europe a special variety of walnut, the Manchurian walnut, *Juglans mandshurica,* can be grown. *Juglans nigra,* the black walnut, can be found as a park tree in southern Sweden. Walnut trees like warmth and should be grown in a sheltered position. From Asia the walnut is thought to have spread to southern Europe and from there it has migrated to North America and competes with its native little sister, the pecan nut. Today walnuts are grown commercially in China, the USA and Turkey. But walnuts are grown in many places in Europe for the domestic market. The walnut tree grows in Périgord in southern France, for example. The Périgord truffle is perhaps better known, but when the walnut harvest starts in September, the village markets in the region are full of stalls selling freshly harvested walnuts. They taste quite different from the drier type we eat at Christmas.

Walnuts should be stored in a cool place, preferably in the refrigerator

Healthy and tasty nuts in food

In Spanish almond soup and in vegetarian nut cutlets, almonds and nuts are actually the main ingredients. But in most of the recipes in this book nuts are used as a flavour enhancer and to give a dish that little extra something. In a salad of easily-chewed vegetables, a few crunchy nuts can considerably enhance the eating experience. Just the flavour of toasted chopped almonds, can raise a fish dish to unimagined heights. In the Middle East and the countries around the Mediterranean, the food often includes nuts and almonds. We have a tradition of serving different sauces with meat and fish as we think they're too dry and tasteless otherwise. These sauces often contain cream and butter and they help to make a meal delicious, but perhaps unnecessarily fatty. In the Mediterranean countries there are a lot of different kinds of garnish used in the same way as we use our beloved sauces. The base is almonds, pine nuts or maybe walnuts, which are ground, seasoned in various ways to suit the dish and lengthened with olive oil. A delicious alternative containing a better balance of healthy fats.

Nuts contain a lot of fat, that is why they should be stored in a cool place, some nuts even in the refrigerator. The oil in the nuts quite simply turns rancid otherwise. You've probably bitten into a bitter nut at some time and that means it was probably stored wrongly. But nuts, above all hazelnuts, walnuts and almonds, as we have said, contain mainly healthy fats, what we call mono-unsaturated and poly-unsaturated fats. Nuts also contain omega-3 fatty acids and omega-6 fatty acids, which are among the essential nutrients which the body cannot manufacture itself, but must obtain. Omega-3 is found among other things in fatty fish, rapeseed oil and walnuts and omega-6 is found in abundance in avocados, almonds, pine nuts, sunflower seeds and sesame seeds.

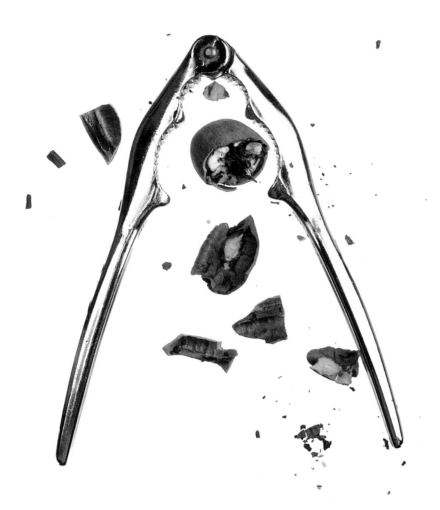

Also nuts do not contain cholesterol and there are studies showing that macadamia nuts even help to lower the cholesterol level in the blood. Nuts also contain a lot of vitamin E, magnesium and zinc. We are actually rarely deficient in vitamin E, *tocopherol,* but it might be interesting to know that it helps the body's acid absorption and can prevent leg cramps and workout pains and lower the blood pressure. Vitamin E can also help burn off fat.

I have a drawer in the fridge full of lots of different kinds of nuts which are easy to bring out and brighten up my meals. I recommend you to do the same.

Look at the list on pages 140 and 141 too, which sets out the nutritional value of each individual nut.

Nut allergies

There is a downside to nuts and almonds, however.

Two close friends of mine, Anna and Sara, are enormously allergic to nuts. They always carry an adrenalin syringe and cortisone tablets with them in their handbags. For them a flake of hazelnut may be life-threatening. Since we don't need to eat nuts to survive, they can enjoy life anyway, but the anxiety is always present when they are invited out or if anyone offers them a piece of chocolate. Dare I, what's in that?

I have great sympathy for all those with nut allergies as it's not a nice situation to be excluded from something which most people take for granted. Nuts, almonds and seeds are extremely common causes of allergy. This may express itself in somewhat different ways, from life-threatening anaphylactic shock, which is an acute hypersensitivity reaction involving several organ functions simultaneously including the heart function and blood pressure, down to an itch in the mouth, eczema, runny eyes, stomach ache and vomiting and/or nettle-rash. You can become allergic to nuts at any time of life.

Find out if there are any people with nut allergy among your friends. Most people can eat pine nuts and coconuts, which are not actually nuts, but ask first. When your friends who have a nut allergy come round, you can serve the nuts in a bowl a little way away from the other food so that there are no unnecessary complications. Or just leave out the nuts completely.

100 recipes with nutritious nuts

Spicy macadamias

Are you one of those people who has discovered macadamia nuts and gone crazy for them? In that case you're not alone.

1 tbsp neutral cooking oil

1 tbsp sugar

1 tsp curry powder

1 tsp cumin

1 tsp coriander

1 pinch or more of chilli

1 tsp sea salt

300 g macadamia nuts

1. Set the oven to 200°C. Spread a sheet of greaseproof paper on a baking tray.

2. Place the oil, sugar and all the seasonings in a bowl, add the nuts and stir.

3. Lay the nuts on the tray and roast them for a little while in the oven until they begin to smell good and the nuts have a good colour. Remove the baking tray from the oven and allow the nuts to cool.

Warning! Never eat a nut directly from the oven. Nuts have the ability to absorb heat and store it and it takes quite a while before they cool down. You can really burn your mouth if you are not careful.

Pistachio nuts with aniseed

I've tried this with Greek ouzo, which works well too, but you need to add 1 tbsp sugar. You can try it with different nuts and other flavoursome liqueurs.

300 g pistachio nuts

1 tbsp neutral cooking oil

2 tbsp Sambuca or another aniseed-flavoured liqueur

1 tsp sea salt

2 tsp whole aniseed

1. Just pour all the ingredients into a saucepan, bring to the boil and simmer until almost all the liquid has evaporated.

2. Continue to simmer until the nuts begin to turn brown. Tip them on to a dish and leave to cool before serving.

Salted roasted almonds

The simplest way is to roast almonds and nuts on a baking tray in the oven, especially if you want to roast a large quantity in one go.

300 g almonds
1-2 tbsp neutral cooking oil
1-3 tsp. sea salt

Set the oven to 200°C. Mix the oil and salt together in a bowl, add the unpeeled almonds and stir. Spread the almonds on a baking tray covered with greaseproof paper and roast them for about 10 minutes or until the nuts begin to crackle and smell good.

Spicy almonds

200 g sweet almonds
1-2 tbsp neutral cooking oil
Sea salt
Chilli

Shell and blanch the almonds. Toast them in a moderately hot, dry frying pan until they begin to crackle and turn colour. Pour in the oil and stir. Season with salt and chilli.

Tips! You can of course use your own favourite seasoning in the mix and create your own spiced nuts.

Bruschetta with chicken liver paté and walnuts

SERVES 4

4 slices of unsweetened
bruschetta or farmhouse loaf
Olive oil
2 cloves of garlic
Chicken liver paté (see p. 33)
Walnuts

1. Set the oven to 225°C. Cut the slices of bread in half if they are large. Place them on a baking tray covered with greaseproof paper. Pour a little oil over them and toast them in the oven until they start to turn golden brown around the edges.

2. Split the garlic cloves through the middle and rub the garlic into one side of each slice of bread. Spread with the paté and sprinkle a few walnuts over them. Eat immediately.

In some places in Germany a peasant farmer could only marry after he had planted a number of walnut trees. A really lovely dowry!

Small tortillas with potatoes, leeks and almonds

If you have a small frying pan you can make the tortilla in that. Otherwise you will need to use a big pan and cut it into smaller pieces. This recipe is designed for a small pan, so double the quantities if you are using a big one.

SERVES 4

2 eggs

Olive oil

1 potato, sliced

1 small length of leek, shredded

8 almonds

Salt and pepper

1. Whisk the eggs. Heat the oil in the pan, add the potato, leek and almonds, leave them to sizzle a little. Stir. Pour over the beaten egg, drag a fork across the pan a few times and reduce the heat.

2. When the tortilla has begun to set and is almost ready, it's time to use a saucepan lid. Place the lid on the pan, turn the tortilla out on to the lid and slide it back into the pan to finish frying on the other side. Season with salt and pepper. Leave to cool, divide the tortilla into four and serve.

Serrano ham with Manchego cheese and walnuts

ABOUT 20 NIBBLES

20 thin slices of Serrano ham

2-3 mandarins (20 segments)

200 g Manchego cheese

About 20 walnuts

Cocktail sticks

Peel the mandarins, divide them into segments. Cut the cheese into 20 sticks. Spread out slices of ham, place a mandarin segment, a cheese stick and a walnut on each slice, roll up and skewer with a cocktail stick.

Prawns, garlic and almonds

If you have ovenproof tapas dishes made of glazed clay, you can serve the prawns in those.

100 ml rapeseed oil

1 tsp chilli pepper flakes

10 garlic cloves, sliced

30 almonds with their skin

200 g shelled prawns (400 g shell-on)

Heat the oil in a high-sided frying pan. Place the chilli, garlic and almonds in the pan and stir. When the garlic begins to brown it's time to add the prawns. Heat them through quickly and serve immediately in small bowls, with bread.

Antipasto platter with nuts

An extremely simple starter, which encourages conversation whilst picking at these tasty morsels. This is just a suggestion, you may have your own favourites.

Sun-dried ham

Salami

Sliced liver sausage

A hard cheese

Various kinds of olives

Gherkins

Radishes

Walnuts

Toasted almonds (see p. 25)

Toasted hazelnuts (see p. 25)

Use a big serving platter or a pretty tray. Arrange each type of meat separately, the cheese separately, the vegetables and nuts separately. Offer everyone small plates and cocktail sticks and enjoy the moment.

Mussels with curry and pine nuts

SERVES 4

500 g frozen mussels with shells

3 cloves of garlic

1-2 tbsp curry powder

Grated zest of ½ lemon

Salt and pepper

25 g butter, at room temperature

Juice of ½ lemon

50 g pine nuts

Set the oven to 225°C. Split open the mussels and place the half shells with the mussels on an ovenproof dish. Squeeze the garlic directly into a bowl, mix in the curry powder, lemon peel, salt and pepper. Stir in the butter. Place a small dab of butter on each mussel, squeeze over a little lemon juice, sprinkle with the nuts and place in the oven for 10-15 minutes. Serve the mussels lukewarm.

Tips! In well-stocked shops you can usually get olives stuffed with almonds, which you can just tip into a bowl and serve.

Grapefuit with tiger prawns and pine nuts

SERVES 4

12 tiger prawns

2 pink grapefruit

2 avocados

½ packet deep frozen petit pois

A few mixed lettuce leaves

50 g pine nuts

Dressing

Juice of ½ lemon

3 tbsp rapeseed oil

Dill

Salt and pepper

1. Start by mixing the dressing. Thaw and peel the prawns. Divide the grapefruit and cut the segments between the membranes. Cut out the white membranes from the grapefruit halves

2. Cut the avocados in half and scoop them out, thaw the peas by rinsing in cold water.

3. Place a little lettuce in the bottom of the grapefruit skins. Divide the prawns, grapefruit segments, pieces of avocado and peas between the skins. Sprinkle the dressing over them, scatter the pine nuts on top and serve.

Parma ham with cheese and nut cream

A starter which is quick to prepare.

SERVES 4

1-2 stems of celery

12 slices of Parma ham or other air-dried ham

12 small lettuce leaves

Cheese and nut cream

100 g ricotta cheese

50 g finely chopped pecan nuts or walnuts

Salt and pepper

1. Start with the cream and mix together the ricotta, nuts, salt and pepper in a bowl. Cut the celery into thin sticks about 10 cm long.

2. Spread out the ham slices, place a lettuce leaf, a couple of celery sticks and a dab of nut cream on one end of the ham and roll up. The lettuce and celery may stick out at one end. Arrange the ham rolls on a platter. Ready to serve!

If you suffer from a bad back, sciatica or rheumatic pain, it helps to have an unshelled walnut in your pocket. At any rate that's according to an old wives tale!

Pissaladière with pine nuts and thyme

A French variation on tarte à l'oignon or onion quiche but much tastier. It sounds like an awful lot of onion, but it's surprising to see how little there really is when the onion has cooked down.

½ packet of yeast
200 ml water
2 tbsp olive oil at room temperature
1 tsp honey
400 – 500 ml self-raising flour

6-7 onions
Olive oil
1 tin of anchovies
Small black olives
1 tbsp dried thyme
Pine nuts

1. Crumble the yeast into a bowl, warm the water and dissolve the yeast in it. Pour in the oil and honey. Work in the flour a little at a time, to make a smooth dough. Leave to prove for an hour, away from any draughts.

2. During this time peel the onions. Cut them in very thin slices and fry gently in the oil in a frying pan. It takes about 35 minutes. The onion should begin to turn golden but must not be browned.

3. Take out the dough and knead. Roll it out thinly into a large rectangle which almost covers a baking tray. Place it on a baking tray lined with greaseproof paper. Brush with olive oil.

4. Spread the onion over the dough and arrange the anchovies in a pattern, if necessary splitting them lengthwise. Decorate with olives. Leave to rise for another 30 minutes. Set the oven to 225°C. Sprinkle on the thyme and bake for about 20 minutes. Take the pissaladière out of the oven, scatter the pine nuts over it and bake for a further 5-10 minutes or until the pine nuts have turned a fine golden colour. Cut into pieces and serve warm.

Chicken liver paté

About 200 g chicken liver
2 shallots, chopped
1 clove of garlic, sliced
6 mushrooms, roughly chopped or sliced
1 tsp rosemary
1 tsp thyme
1 tsp sage
2 tbsp balsamic vinegar
1 tbsp Japanese soy sauce
50 ml light crème fraîche
Salt and pepper

1. Drain the liver on kitchen paper. Sauté the onion, garlic and mushrooms first and reserve on a plate. Then sauté the liver until it is almost cooked through and season with the rosemary, thyme and sage. Add the onion and mushrooms. Pour on the vinegar and soy sauce and simmer to reduce the liquid. Leave the mixture to cool a little.

2. Place the liver mixture in a food processor together with the crème fraîche. Blend to a smooth consistency. Season to taste with salt and pepper. Leave to cool.

Gado gado salad

Despite its simple ingredients, this Indonesian salad is a real gourmet dish. A cheese slice is a useful utensil in preparing this dish.

SERVES 4

¼ of a white cabbage

1 cucumber

5 medium boiled potatoes, sliced

4 hard-boiled eggs, quartered

200 g fresh or canned bean sprouts

100 g chopped roasted peanuts

Chives

Dressing with peanuts

200 g roasted peanuts

2 tbsp peanut butter

200 ml coconut milk

2 tbsp lime juice

2 tbsp neutral cooking oil

2 garlic cloves

1 tsp ground coriander

Salt

1. Start with the dressing. Finely chop the peanuts or grind them in the blender. Mix them with the peanut butter, coconut milk, lime juice, oil, crushed garlic and coriander to form a smooth sauce. Season with salt.

2. Take a large platter, shred the cabbage with the cheese slice so that it is very finely shredded. Continue by slicing the cucumber thinly over the cabbage in the same way. Peel the potatoes and eggs, slice the potatoes and quarter the eggs and arrange on the salad. Scatter the bean sprouts over. Sprinkle the dressing on, scatter the nuts and chives over the salad.

Artichoke salad

This has three of my top favourite ingredients: oranges, artichokes and roasted nuts. A wonderfully tasty salad which is best presented on a large serving dish. Artichokes are in the shops from July to April. Peel the oranges with a knife so that all the white pith comes off as well.

SERVES 4

1 head of radicchio, torn into small pieces

400 g cooked Jerusalem artichokes, sliced

2 peeled and sliced oranges

½ red onion, thinly sliced

50 g pine nuts

1 punnet of cress

Dressing

Juice of ½ lemon

3 tbsp olive oil

Salt and coarsely ground black pepper

Mix the dressing. Take a large serving dish. Scatter the lettuce and arrange slices of artichoke, orange and red onion over it. Sprinkle with the dressing. Scatter the nuts and finally cut the cress and place it on top.

The Norwegian Thorbjørn Egner wrote the book about Klas Klatremus and the other animals in Hackeback Forest in the early fifties. In addition to being an author, Egner was also a draughtsman and graphic artist and illustrated his books himself. In Hackeback Forest the animals live in a world reminiscent of our own. Some save nuts and store them up for a hard winter; others don't bother and instead live for the moment. In the bushes the fox lies in wait for a good meal and he's not interested in nuts ...

Waldorf salad

*I've never eaten the salad in the famous
New York hotel but I do know one thing.
It's important to choose good flavoursome
and slightly sour apples, ideally two
different varieties.*

4 GENEROUS SERVINGS

200 g celeriac

3 apples

1 tbsp lemon juice

100 ml mayonnaise

3 tbsp single cream

1 tbsp grated lemon peel

Salt and black pepper

Colourful mixed salad leaves

50 g nice-looking shelled walnuts

1. Peel and cut the celeriac in slices and
   blanch it in lightly salted water. Cool
   immediately by rinsing under cold water.
   Leave it to drain and cut it into small sticks.

2. Rinse and cut all the apples into sticks,
   place them in a bowl of cold water and
   pour on the lemon juice so that they don't
   turn brown.

3. Mix together the mayonnaise, cream, lemon
   juice, salt and pepper. Place the lettuce
   leaves on four plates, divide the celeriac
   and apples between them, pour over the
   dressing and sprinkle on the nuts.

Crisp green salad with hazelnuts

You can use a few different kinds of leaves, it's important for some of them to be a little bitter so that there is a good contrast between the sharp, the bitter and the slightly sweet flavours.

SERVES 4

2-3 chicory heads depending on size

Rocket

Red lettuce or radicchio

2 cooking apples

A little lemon juice

150 g goats cheese

50 – 100 g roasted hazelnuts, coarsely chopped

Dressing

Juice of ½ grapefruit

3 tbsp hazelnut oil

½ tbsp honey

Salt and pepper

1. Mix the dressing first. It's a good idea to arrange the salad directly on four individual plates, dividing up the leaves first.

2. Peel the apples and slice them. Place the slices in a bowl of water with a little lemon juice so that they don't turn brown.

3. Cut or break the goats' cheese into bite-sized pieces. Arrange the apple slices and cheese on the salad leaves, sprinkle on the dressing and scatter over the nuts.

Tips! If your honey is not runny, put however much honey you need in a stainless steel measure. Place the measure over a warm burner until the honey is runny, then it's easy to mix into the dressing.

Salad with oyster mushrooms and Brazil nuts, with salsa

This tastes best if the mushrooms are slightly warm.

SERVES 4

100 g Brazil nuts

300 g oyster mushrooms

Rapeseed oil and butter

2 shallots

2 stems of celery

½ small courgette

3 stalks of parsley

8 fresh sage leaves

1 well rinsed curly lettuce

Salsa

100 ml extra virgin olive oil

Juice of ½ lemon

1 clove of garlic

Salt and pepper

1. Set the oven to 200°C. Chop the nuts coarsely and roast them in the oven for about 10 minutes. Leave them to cool. Tear the mushrooms into strips, fry them in a little rapeseed oil and add a small dab of butter, season with salt and pepper.

2. Measure the olive oil into a bowl, mix with the lemon juice, chopped or crushed garlic, season with salt and pepper. Chop the onion, celery, courgette, parsley and sage finely and add to the dressing. Finely chop the nuts and mix them into the salsa, if necessary season with more salt and pepper.

3. Tear the lettuce into pieces, place on a serving dish, add the mushrooms and pour the salsa over.

Green bean salad with roasted almonds

A refreshing salad which can be served with a little cold meat or poultry for example.

SERVES 4

200 g cooked cold green beans

50 g peeled roasted almonds

½ bunch parsley, finely chopped

½ bunch chives, finely chopped

1 lemon

Dressing

50 ml olive oil

Juice of ½ lemon

1 clove of garlic

Salt and pepper

1. Prepare the dressing first. Place the beans, almonds, parsley and chives in a bowl. Rinse the lemon and cut it first in slices then each slice into quarters.

2. Mix the lemon pieces into the bean mixture and pour the dressing over. It's good to let the salad stand and marinate at room temperature for about half an hour before it is eaten.

A famous work of art of our time is Wilhelm Tell by Salvador Dali, painted in 1933, which is housed at the Museum of Modern Art in Stockholm. People probably don't notice the little walnut shell at first, since the picture is big and the main motif is so striking: a man with an enormously extended buttock, like some grotesque growth. Behind one of his feet lies a walnut shell and perhaps there is a little figure inside the shell!

Ajo blanco

This cold soup made of almonds and garlic is something to eat on a hot summer's day. A cousin of the famous gazpacho you might say, but with no other similarity than that it is of Spanish origin and is served cold. I usually don't strain the soup because I think it's nicer as it is.

SERVES 4

2 – 3 slices of unsweetened white bread, toasted

3 peeled cloves of garlic

200 g blanched shelled almonds

1 tsp salt

100 ml mild olive oil

50 ml sherry vinegar

300 g white seedless grapes or grapes with the seeds removed

1. Soak the bread in a little water. Blend the almonds, garlic, bread, salt and olive oil in a food processor. Add the vinegar a little at a time, tasting as you go. You may not need the whole quantity.

2. The soup can then be strained and diluted to the required consistency with water. Cut the grapes in half and place in the soup when serving or serve them separately in a bowl.

Asian soup with noodles and roasted peanuts

In the Vietnamese kitchen roasted peanuts are used a lot.

4 stems of lemon grass
1 litre water
2 vegetable stock cubes
2 garlic cloves, chopped
3 cm fresh ginger, grated
½ bunch fresh coriander

1 packet quick-cook noodles
2 cm leek, shredded
100 g bean sprouts
4 radishes, sliced
Chopped peanuts

1. Cut the lemon grass off just above the thick part and peel away the outer woody layers. Beat it with the back of a knife handle so that it splits into fibres. Bring the water, stock cubes, garlic, lemon grass, ginger and coriander to the boil. Simmer for about 10 minutes. Strain the stock and throw away the spices.

2. Bring the stock to the boil again, add the noodles and boil until they are transparent. Divide the soup between individual bowls and add the leek, bean sprouts and radishes. Serve chopped peanuts separately so that everyone can help themselves.

Savoy cabbage soup with chicken balls and hazelnuts

A simple, economical and delicious soup which is also very easy to make.

SERVES 4

½ head of Savoy cabbage, shredded

10 cm leek, shredded

Neutral cooking oil

800 ml water

2 tbsp concentrated chicken stock

Possibly a little soy sauce

100 g roasted hazelnuts

Chicken balls

200 g chicken mince

1 clove of garlic

1 tsp lemon thyme

Salt and pepper

1. Start with the chicken balls. Place the mince in a bowl and crush the garlic into it. Add the thyme and season with salt and pepper. Stir. Form into small balls, about the size of a cherry.

2. Sauté the shredded cabbage and leek in a little oil in a pan or large saucepan. Add the water and chicken stock, bring to the boil and add the chicken balls. Simmer for about 15 minutes, season with salt and pepper and possibly a few dashes of soy sauce.

3. Place the roasted chopped nuts in a bowl and serve with the soup.

Prawn soup with roasted almonds

SERVES 4

500 g prawns with shell

3 finely chopped shallots

1 finely chopped clove of garlic

1 piece finely chopped celeriac

Olive oil

2 tbsp flour

300 ml white wine

500 ml fish stock

1 tin whole tomatoes

Salt and pepper

Tabasco

Flaked roasted almonds

1. Peel the prawns but keep the shells. Sauté all the onion and celeriac in the oil in a large pan. Add the prawn shells, stir and sprinkle on the flour, add the wine, stock and tomatoes. Put the lid on and simmer the soup for about 15 minutes.

2. Remove the prawns and vegetables and bring the soup to the boil again, season with salt, pepper and possibly a few dashes of Tabasco. Divide the prawns between individual dishes, pour the hot soup over them and sprinkle generously with flaked almonds.

Creamy artichoke soup with red caviar and roasted hazelnuts

SERVES 4

6-7 Jerusalem artichokes

1 parsnip

2 potatoes

3 shallots, sliced

Oil

200 ml white wine

2 tbsp concentrated chicken stock

500 – 600 ml water

4 tbsp crème fraîche

4 tbsp red caviar

2 tbsp chives, chopped

100 g roasted hazelnuts, chopped

1. Peel the root vegetables, cut them in pieces and boil them in a little water in a big pan until they begin to go mushy. Fry the onion in a little oil, pour on the wine and chicken stock. Strain off the water from the vegetables into another pan or measuring jug.

2. Put the onion, wine and stock into the pan with the vegetables and blend them with a hand-held blender or use the food processor. Measure the vegetable stock and add water to make up 500 ml. Thin the soup with the stock, gradually, until it is the right creamy consistency. If necessary heat it again.

3. Pour the soup into bowls. Add a dash of crème fraîche and a dab of caviar to the middle of each bowl, sprinkle with chives and hazelnuts and serve.

Cannelloni with Jerusalem artichokes and cashew nuts

You can use a ready-made tomato sauce which you like or make this very simple version.

SERVES 4

12 cannelloni tubes
1 batch artichoke filling (see below)
1 batch tomato sauce (see below)
Parmesan cheese

1. Set the oven to 225°C. Fill the tubes with the filling as follows. Use a teaspoon and fill from one end and press down a little with the spoon. Turn and fill the rest of the tube from the other end.

2. Place the tubes in an ovenproof dish, pour the tomato sauce over and sprinkle with grated Parmesan cheese. Place in the oven for 30 minutes with aluminium foil over, then remove the foil and bake for a further 10 minutes.

Filling
150 g Jerusalem artichokes, 3-4 chokes
2 shallots
100 g smoked ham
8 sage leaves
100 g ricotta cheese
Black pepper
100 g chopped roasted cashew nuts

1. Peel and boil the artichokes in a little water until they are soft. Cut them into small pieces, finely chop the shallots and chop the ham fairly small. Fry all these ingredients in a little oil in a frying pan until the onion is soft and slightly coloured.

2. Mix in the finely chopped sage and the ricotta cheese. Pepper and finally stir in the cashew nuts.

Tomato sauce

1 onion

1 clove garlic

Olive oil

1 tin tomatoes, chopped

200 ml water

1 vegetable stock cube

Chop the onion and garlic. Fry in a little olive oil, add the tomatoes, water and crumble the stock cube over. Bring to the boil and simmer the sauce for 10 minutes.

Conchiglie with tomato sauce, aubergine and almonds

A delicious pasta sauce which is quick to make.

SERVES 4

1 aubergine

Salt

Olive oil

2 cloves garlic

2 tins whole tomatoes

1 vegetable stock cube

400 g conchiglie or similar pasta

10 basil leaves

150 g ricotta cheese

100 blanched and roasted almonds

1. Slice the aubergines, salt and leave to sweat for 10-15 minutes. Rinse off the slices in water, dry on kitchen paper and fry the slices in oil. Leave the slices to drain on kitchen paper. Then cut the cooled slices into strips about 1 cm wide.

2. Slice the garlic and fry in a little oil. Pour on the tomatoes, crumble the stock cube over and leave the sauce to simmer gently without a lid for about 10 minutes.

3. Cook the pasta according to the instructions on the packet. Drain in a colander and rinse quickly with cold water.

4. Add the aubergine and basil to the sauce. Divide the pasta between individual deep plates, pour over the hot sauce, crumble the ricotta cheese on top and sprinkle with almonds.

Pasta sauce with spinach and roasted walnuts

A delicious pasta sauce which is quick to make.

SERVES 4

200 g frozen chopped spinach

100 ml light crème fraîche

1 vegetable stock cube

100 g chopped roasted walnuts

75 g creamy blue cheese

Salt and pepper

400 g pasta, such as farfalle

1. Thaw the spinach over a low heat in a saucepan on the hob, add the crème fraîche and stock cube, stir and bring to the boil.

2. Add the nuts and cheese and warm through until the cheese has melted. Season with salt and pepper. Cook the pasta in accordance with the instructions on the packet and serve immediately, with the sauce.

Spaghetti with anchovies and pine nuts

A delicious salty sauce or paté which tastes great with a big glass of beer. I usually rinse the anchovies in a little water before I use them but anchovy experts say that is sacrilege!

SERVES 4

Sauce

3 onions

Olive oil

Butter

1 bunch finely chopped flat-leaved parsley

1 small can finely chopped anchovies

50 g pine nuts

400 g spaghetti

Grated Parmesan cheese

1. Peel and slice the onions and fry them until they are soft over a medium heat in a mixture of olive oil and butter. Add the parsley and anchovies.

2. Simmer the mixture carefully for a while. Cook the spaghetti according to the instructions on the packet. Add the pine nuts to the sauce and serve with the steaming hot pasta. Serve with grated Parmesan cheese separately.

Pasta with tomato sauce, prawns and pistachio nuts

It's a good idea to use the kind of pasta known as gemelli ('twins') or strozzapreti (priests' collars) or macaroni or some other kind which absorbs the sauce well.

SERVES 4

Tomato sauce

2 onions

4 cloves garlic

Olive oil

2 tins whole tomatoes

1 vegetable stock cube

1 red pepper

1 tbsp balsamic vinegar

1 tsp chilli pepper

50 g chopped oregano or 1 tbsp dried

250 g peeled prawns (500 g with shell)

400 g pasta

50 g pistachio nuts

Grated Parmesan cheese

1. Peel and chop the onion, peel and slice the garlic and fry in oil in a saucepan or large high-sided frying pan. Pour on the tomatoes, crumble in the stock cube, bring to the boil and leave to simmer for about 5 minutes.

2. Chop the pepper and add to the sauce. Season with vinegar, chilli pepper and oregano. Leave to simmer for about 10 minutes more. Add the prawns at the end but they must not boil, just be warmed through. Cook the pasta according to the instructions on the packet. Serve immediately with the sauce, pistachio nuts and grated Parmesan cheese.

How about zander

Zander is a fantastic fish which is even more delicious cooked in a flavoursome packet like this. Perfect for putting on the barbecue in the summer but just as nice the rest of the year – cooked in the oven.

4 zander fillets weighing 150 – 200 g each

2 bulbs of fennel

20 cocktail tomatoes

8 spring onions or young leeks

1 bunch dill

Salt and pepper

200 ml apple juice

Butter

100 g roasted cashew nuts

Aluminium foil

1. Set the oven to 225°C. Wash all the vegetables. Remove the woody parts of the fennel and cut into thin slices or shred. Divide the spring onions into smaller slivers or shred the leek.

2. Spread four sheets of foil and divide the fennel, tomatoes, onion and dill between them. Place the fish on top and season with salt and pepper.

3. Fold up the edges of the foil and pour 50 ml apple juice on to each packet, add a dab of butter and sprinkle on the nuts. Close the foil packets carefully with the seam on top. Place the packets in a roasting dish in the oven for 20 – 30 minutes. You can take a look in one packet after 20 minutes to see whether the fish is opaque, white and firm in the flesh. When it is it's ready to eat.

Herring fillets with lemon and pine nuts

A delicious herring recipe which makes you think of the Mediterranean.

SERVES 4

1 bunch dill, finely chopped

1 bunch parsley, finely chopped

Grated rind of 1 lemon

2 cloves of garlic, fincly chopped

50 – 100 g pine nuts

Salt and pepper

1 kg herring, filleted

Olive oil and butter

1. Mix together the dill, parsley, lemon peel, garlic, pine nuts, salt and pepper in a bowl.

2. Divide the filling between half of the herring fillets and place the remaining fillets on top. Fry the sandwiched fillets and serve immediately with freshly boiled potatoes and lemon wedges.

Oven baked plaice with red butter

SERVES 4

4 small or 2 large plaice

Salt and pepper

Red butter

75 g butter

1 red onion, finely chopped

50 g pickled beetroot, chopped

100 g hazelnuts, chopped

Salt and pepper

1. Set the oven to 100°C. Lay the plaice in a big roasting dish with the back uppermost, season with salt and pepper and cook them in the oven for about 30 minutes. Remove and raise the temperature to 200°C. Loosen the skin from the fish.

2. While the fish is in the oven, beat the butter, which is easiest to work with if it is at room temperature. Fry the onion in a little butter in a frying pan until it is soft and mix with the beetroot and half the hazelnuts in a bowl. Mash the butter into the mix, season with salt and pepper.

3. Place a dab of butter on each plaice, sprinkle with the remaining hazelnuts and place in the oven until the butter has melted and the nuts have a good colour, about 10 minutes.

Scampi with pesto gratin

Serve as a hot dish with a generous salad and good bread or use half the quantity and serve the scampi as an entrée.

SERVES 4

16 large cooked scampi or Pacific prawns

About 100 g classic Genovese pesto
(see page 94)

Lemon

1. Set the oven to 250°C. Split the scampi and chop the flesh roughly. Mix with the pesto
2. Place the empty shells in an ovenproof dish and divide the filling between the shells, squeeze a little lemon juice over. Grill for about 10 minutes in the centre of the oven and serve immediately.

Fish au gratin with an almond coating

This is an old classic which has stood the test of time well. Very popular with children and easy to make. A salad of grated carrot and a little lemon juice and green peas are my favourite accompaniments to this fish dish. The recipe is easy to remember because it takes 50 millilitres of everything except the fish.

SERVES 3

1 block of frozen fish, haddock, coley or cod

400 – 500 g

Salt and pepper

50 ml mayonnaise

50 ml chilli sauce

50 ml breadcrumbs

50 ml almonds, finely chopped

50 ml flaked almonds

1. Set the oven to 200°C. Place the fish in an ovenproof dish. Season with salt and pepper. Mix together the mayonnaise, chilli sauce, breadcrumbs and chopped almonds and spread over the fish.

2. Place aluminium foil over the dish and cook in the oven for 50 minutes. Remove the foil, raise the oven temperature to 225°C. Sprinkle the flaked almonds over and put the fish back in the oven for about 10 minutes or until the almonds are a nice golden colour and the fish is cooked through.

Turkey fillet with walnut and gorgonzola filling

Turkey, like chicken, is a very rewarding meat which marries well with almost any other flavours. This dish particularly does justice to the flavour of this lean meat, with gorgonzola and walnuts. It's good with fresh pasta.

SERVES 4 – 6

2 turkey breast fillets weighing 250 – 350 g each

Salt and pepper

150 g gorgonzola

100 g walnuts

Oil

Cocktail sticks

1. Set the oven to 200°C. Cut a slit in each fillet from the side. Season inside the pockets with salt and pepper and stuff with gorgonzola and the nuts.

2. Close the pocket using the cocktail sticks and place the fillets, seam up, in an ovenproof dish. Baste with oil, season with salt and pepper and bake in the lower half of the oven for about 30 minutes.

Chicken with coconut

A delicious Asian dish with just the right hotness and plenty of flavour. Try it with black beans and rice.

SERVES 4

About 1 kg chicken thighs

Salt and pepper

Sesame oil + a neutral oil

1 leek, shredded

4 cloves of garlic, sliced

1 red chilli

3 cm fresh ginger

2 stalks of lemon grass

½ tbsp turmeric

1 tbsp ground coriander

500 ml water

1 can coconut milk, 300 ml

1 vegetable or chicken stock cube

50 g desiccated coconut

Tips! **Lemon grass.** I usually use the bottom part of the stems, the rest of the lemon grass is pretty woody. Use a knife handle and beat the stems thoroughly. The grass gets softer and the flavour comes out better.

1. Season the chicken thighs with salt and pepper and fry until they are golden in a mixture of sesame oil and a neutral oil. Transfer them to a saucepan.

2. Sauté the leek and garlic, transfer to the saucepan. Cut the chilli lengthwise, remove the seeds and the white pith and shred. Grate the ginger and crush the stems of the lemon grass. Place everything in the saucepan with the chicken, together with the turmeric and coriander.

3. Pour on the water and coconut milk, crumble the stock cube over. Stir and bring to the boil, then simmer for about 20 minutes or until the chicken is cooked through.

4. Roast the coconut in a dry pan and serve as an accompaniment in a separate bowl.

Chicken casserole
with olives and almonds

A great dish to serve your guests which you can make in a lovely big roasting dish or casserole in the oven. Serve with tasty bread.

SERVES 6 – 8

2 fresh chickens

Salt and pepper

Butter and olive oil

150 g bacon, in thin strips

300 g peeled pickling onions or shallots

1 tbsp thyme

1 bottle dry white wine

1 can green olives, possibly flavoured with lemon

½ bunch parsley, chopped

2 bay leaves

2 vegetable or chicken stock cubes

100 g roasted unblanched almonds

1. Set the oven to 200°C. Cut the chicken into pieces, season with salt and pepper. Brown the chicken pieces in a frying pan with butter and olive oil. Add the strips of bacon. When the meat has browned it's time to place it in the oven dish together with the bacon.

2. Brown the onion with the thyme in the frying pan and transfer to the oven dish.

3. Pour over the wine, add the olives, parsley and bay leaves and crumble the stock cubes over. Bake in the oven for about 45 minutes. Test a fleshy part of the chicken with a skewer and check that the liquid which runs out is clear, which means it's done.

4. Take the dish or pan out of the oven and place the
   almonds on a baking tray. Roast for about 10 minutes.
   Sprinkle the almonds over the chicken casserole
   and serve.

Chicken kebabs with peanut sauce

Peanut sauce is a favourite with many people. It's a good idea to serve a crisp green salad with this.

SERVES 4

4 chicken fillets

Oil

Salt and pepper

12 dampened bamboo skewers

Peanut sauce

2 cloves of garlic

2 shallots

1 tbsp ground nut oil or rapeseed oil

100 g peanut butter

100 g roasted peanuts, coarsely chopped

1 tbsp honey

200 ml coconut milk

Salt and chilli pepper

1. Chop the garlic and shallots finely, sauté in oil in a saucepan until the onions are soft and slightly coloured.

2. Add the peanut butter, peanuts, honey and 150 ml coconut milk. Leave to simmer for about 10 minutes and lengthen with the remaining coconut milk. Season with salt and chilli pepper.

3. Set the oven to 225°C. Cut each chicken fillet into three pieces lengthwise. Thread the meat lengthwise on the skewers. Baste with oil. Season with salt and pepper and place in a baking dish in the oven or grill the kebabs on a barbecue or on a griddle on the hob. Grill/fry the kebabs for 10 - 15 minutes depending on how thick the pieces are. Test one piece and see whether the juices run clear – that's when the kebabs are done. Serve the kebabs with the peanut sauce and salad.

Chicken breasts with pecan nuts and lemon sauce

This chicken casserole has a fantastic lemony flavour. Remember to grate the rind of the lemon before you squeeze the juice out of it, since an "empty" lemon is hard to grate. Serve with broccoli and couscous or wild rice..

SERVES 4

4 chicken breasts

Marinade
Juice of ½ lemon

100 ml water

3 tbsp olive oil

2 cloves garlic, sliced

½ tsp chilli pepper

A few stems of parsley, coarsely chopped

300 ml water

1 chicken stock cube

Grated rind of 1 lemon

½ bunch parsley, finely chopped

1 tbsp dried tarragon or twice as much if fresh

½ tbsp dried lemon thyme or twice as much if fresh

2 tbsp Dijon mustard

½ tbsp honey

Salt and pepper

1 tbsp cornflour

A little water

100 g roasted pecan nuts

1. Cut the chicken fillets into smaller pieces. Mix the marinade in a plastic bag, add the meat and leave to marinade in the refrigerator overnight or at room temperature for a couple of hours.

2. Strain off the marinade but don't throw it away. Dry the meat and fry in a little oil in a pan. Pour on the marinade and simmer for about 5 minutes.

3. Add the water, stock cube, lemon peel and herbs. Bring to the boil and simmer for 10 minutes. Stir in the mustard and honey, bring to the boil, season with salt and pepper. Blend the cornflour with a little water, pour it into the pan, bring to the boil, stirring all the time. Sprinkle with the pecan nuts and serve with suitable accompaniments.

Stuffed aubergines

SERVES 4

2 medium aubergines

Stuffing

1 onion

1 - 2 cloves of garlic

250 g minced beef

8 marinaded sun-dried tomatoes

100 g roasted salted peanuts

½ bunch parsley

1 tbsp fennel seeds

2 tbsp tomato purée

Salt and pepper

Olive oil for basting

200 ml boiling water

A little salt

1. Rinse and roll the aubergines backwards and forwards on a chopping board until they feel soft. Cut about a 2 cm 'cap' off at the stalk ends, scoop out the flesh both from the cap and the rest of the aubergine. Salt the inside of the caps and the aubergines. Stand them upside down on kitchen paper. Chop the flesh from the aubergines coarsely.

2. Chop the onion and garlic finely. Fry the onion and garlic in oil in a frying pan, add the mince and simmer until it is cooked through. Finely chop the tomatoes, chop the peanuts and add to the pan. Chop the parsley and add it, together with the chopped aubergine, fennel seeds and tomato purée. Add pepper but taste before adding any salt as the peanuts may be sufficient. Bring to the boil and simmer for about 5 minutes. Set the oven to 200°C.

3. Fill the aubergines with the stuffing, press down with the handle of a wooden spoon or similar. They must be well filled and restored to their original shape. Press the caps on.

4. Place the aubergines in an ovenproof dish, pour over the boiling water, cover with aluminium foil and bake in the oven for about 40 minutes.

5. Cut each aubergine half into three or four pieces, serve with oven-roasted root vegetables and a yogurt sauce with chopped almonds and grated cucumber.

Burgers with picada, hazelnuts and cheese

SERVES 4

1 onion

Salt and pepper

500 g minced beef

Butter

Picada (see page 91)

100 g roasted hazelnuts, chopped

4 slices mature cheese

4 slices crusty bread or rolls

1. Chop the onion finely and place in a bowl, sprinkle with salt and pepper and mix with the mince. Form into four thick burgers and fry them in a little butter.

2. Make a pocket in the burgers, place a dab of picada, hazelnuts and cheese in each, serve on the bread or in a roll with lettuce and tomato.

Lamb kebabs with pine nuts

SERVES 4 – 16 KEBABS

1 egg

2 tsp ground cumin

2 tsp ground coriander

Grated peel of ½ lemon

2 cloves garlic

Salt and chilli pepper

½ bunch parsley, finely chopped

100 g roasted pine nuts

800 g minced lamb

Olive oil

Dampened bamboo skewers

1. Set the oven to 225°C. Break the egg into a bowl, add all the spices, lemon peel and crushed garlic. Stir and mix in the finely chopped parsley. Add the pine nuts and minced lamb, a little at a time, until the whole is well mixed.

2. Shape the meat mixture into 'sausages' slightly more than half the length of the skewers. Place the skewers in an ovenproof dish with a little olive oil and roast in the oven for about 30 minutes.

3. Serve the freshly grilled kebabs with a salad made of grated carrot with almonds, raisins and freshly squeezed orange juice. Offer lemon wedges as well.

Entrecôte with hazelnut butter and spring vegetables

SERVES 4

4 finely marbled entrecote steaks

Salt and pepper

Hazelnut butter (see page 89)

Spring vegetables, for example carrots, spring onions, cauliflower, broccoli, sugar snap peas

1. It's a good idea to use a grill plate if you have one or grill on a barbecue if it's the right time of year. The meat is best if it's at room temperature when you start preparing it.

2. Blanch the vegetables briefly, they taste best if they're still a little crunchy. Make sure that the hazelnut butter is not too cold, because it should melt quickly when it is placed on the hot meat.

Beef kebabs with peanuts and rice noodles

I usually serve this kebab with rice noodles, a salad of fresh leek in thin rings with shredded red pepper and a sweet chilli sauce.

SERVES 4

6oo g roast beef or fillet steak

2 shallots

2 cloves of garlic

2 tbsp grated fresh ginger

1 finely shredded red chilli

1 tbsp groundnut oil or rapeseed oil

2 tbsp water

Dampened bamboo skewers cut in half

1oo g roasted peanuts, finely chopped
or crushed

Chilli pepper and salt

Groundnut oil or rapeseed oil

1. Cut the meat into cubes. Chop the shallots and
   garlic finely and place in a bowl with the ginger
   and chilli. Pour over the oil and the water, mix
   and add the meat so that it is covered. Cover
   the bowl, place in the refrigerator for 8 hours
   or overnight. Make sure that the meat is at
   room temperature when you are preparing it.

2. Set the oven to 225°C. Mix together the nuts
   and spices in a large dish with a raised edge.
   Take the meat out of the marinade and lay it in
   the spicy mixture, turning it so that the meat is
   covered with nuts. Thread the cubes on to the
   skewers. Place the kebabs in an oven dish,
   baste with a little oil and place in the oven until
   ready. Or grill the kebabs on a barbecue. Serve
   with noodles, salad and a sweet chilli sauce.

Lamb chops with pistachio coating

Where I buy my lamb you can ask to have butterfly chops split in the middle. It's nice if you're offering dinner outside in the summer and you can serve up a big platter of single chops which everyone can eat with their fingers.

100 g pistachio nuts
100 g breadcrumbs
Salt and pepper
2-3 single chops per person
Oil

Chop the nuts finely in the food processor, mix with breadcrumbs, salt and pepper. Baste the chops with a little oil and grill them first until they are almost done. If necessary coat with a little more oil, turn them in the coating mix and grill them a little longer so that the nuts are slightly browned. Serve with lemon wedges, some good bread and a mixed green salad.

Minute steaks with spring onions, ginger and hazelnuts

The taste of the roasted hazelnuts goes well with the flavours of this dish. I don't usually thicken the sauce but if you want to you can take 1 tablespoon of cornflour mixed with a little water and add this at the end.

SERVES 4

600 g minute steaks

Neutral cooking oil

8 – 10 spring onions in 4 cm long pieces

2 cloves of garlic, finely chopped

300 ml water

½ vegetable stock cube

2 tbsp Japanese soy sauce

1 tbsp balsamic vinegar

2 tbsp grated fresh ginger

2 tomatoes, quartered

1 small packet frozen sugarsnap peas

Chilli pepper

Salt

50 g sliced roasted hazelnuts

1. Cut the meat into strips and toss in a little oil in a pan. Add the spring onions and garlic and sauté together.

2. Add the water, stock cube, soy sauce, vinegar and ginger. Bring the pan to the boil, add the tomatoes, peas and a little chilli, bring to the boil again.

3. Season with a little more salt if necessary. If you like you can thicken the sauce with cornflour. Sprinkle generously with hazelnuts.

Elsa Beskow's fairytales are often set in the forest. In Ocke, Nutta and Pillerill three children get caught up in a crazy adventure high up in the trees on the back of a squirrel. Beskow has armed the children, among other things, with the help of a hazel tree.

In still life paintings nuts are of course common. The Dutch painter Willem Claesz Heda liked to paint still life and one of his paintings, from 1647, shows the remains of a meal. On the table is a pewter dish with leftover fish and shellfish and on the cloth there are whole walnuts, a few hazelnuts and the shells of hazelnuts. The whole picture is in muted colours but the surfaces of the different materials, the silky smooth shell of the hazelnuts, the glinting of the glass and the sparkle of the silver are all beautifully reproduced. The picture hangs in the National Gallery, London.

Nut cutlets

You can of course use whichever nuts you like but this is how I make my nut cutlets. A food processor makes the work as easy as can be.

SERVES 3

200 g walnuts

200 g hazelnuts

1 onion, chopped

2 cloves of garlic, chopped

10 mushrooms, chopped

50 g breadcrumbs

200 g cooked chick peas

50 g parsley, chopped

1 egg

Salt and pepper

Rapeseed oil

Courgette in strips (see page 81)
Romesco sauce (see page 87)

1. Begin by roasting the nuts in the oven or a hot dry frying pan. Grind the nuts in the food processor until they reach the consistency of coarse sand. Toss the onion, garlic and mushrooms in a little oil in a frying pan, season with salt and pepper. Place this mixture with the breadcrumbs, chick peas, parsley, egg, salt and pepper in the food processor. Blend until the mixture is fairly smooth. Leave to stand for about 10 minutes.

2. Heat a little oil in a frying pan. The mixture is fairly soft so place spoonfuls directly into the pan. Flatten the cutlets a little and fry 2 – 3 minutes on each side. Serve them freshly fried with the courgette strips and romesco sauce.

Cauliflower curry with almonds and raisins

This dish goes really well with couscous. And it's a good idea to start with the couscous, because it can stand ready in the saucepan whilst you make the other part. There are various different curry mixes so try them out until you find your favourite and put a little extra curry seasoning on the table for anyone who wants more.

SERVES 4

4 portions couscous

1 orange

1 cauliflower

1 carrot

1 onion

1 red pepper

Oil

1 – 2 tbsp curry

400 ml water

1 vegetable stock cube

50 g raisins

2 tbsp cornflour

Water

1 packet frozen peas or fresh peas

100 g blanched roasted almonds

1. Cook the couscous according to the instructions on the packet. Peel the orange with a sharp knife and cut off all the white pith as well. Cut it into slices or cut out whole segments (see page 106). Stir into the couscous.

2. Break the cauliflower into florets, peel the carrot and cut it into small strips using a cheese slice or potato peeler. Peel and cut the onion into segments and the pepper into bite-sized pieces.

3. Toss the onion in a little oil in a large high-sided frying pan until it is almost soft, sprinkle over the curry powder. Bring the water to the boil with the stock cube, in a saucepan, add the cauliflower and cook for about 5 minutes.

4. Add the carrot strips to the water and simmer for a minute or two more. Pour the stock, cauliflower and carrots over the frying pan. Add the pepper, raisins and peas, bring to the boil. Blend the cornflour with a little water and pour into the curry, stirring all the time. Boil until the liquid thickens. Sprinkle a large handful of roasted almonds over the dish before serving it with the orange couscous.

Courgette in strips with onion, parmesan and pine nuts

SERVES 4

2 courgettes
2 red onions
Olive oil
Salt and pepper
A piece of parmesan cheese
Pine nuts

1. Rinse the courgette and cut it into wide strips with a cheese slice or potato peeler.

2. Place the strips on a large dish. Cut the onion into small segments. Sprinkle over the oil, season with salt and pepper. Slice the parmesan cheese over and sprinkle with pine nuts.

Parsnip quiche with almonds

Parsnips are one of my favourite root vegetables. They have a special flavour which I think is enhanced if you add a little cinnamon.

Follow the recipe for my favourite pastry (see page 83) but replace 50 g flour with 50 g ground almonds. Start by grinding the almonds in the food processor then you just have to add the other ingredients after that.

SERVES 6
Filling

4 cooked parsnips

2 onions

Oil

8 mushrooms, sliced

100 g almonds, coarsely chopped

1 tsp cinnamon

1 can creamed mushrooms

100 ml cream cheese

2 eggs

Salt and pepper

50 ml grated strong cheese

1. Start by making the pastry and put it in the refrigerator. Peel the parsnips, cut them in slices 1 cm thick and boil them lightly, but they mustn't get too soft.

2. Set the oven to 225°C. Peel and slice the onion, fry in a little oil together with the sliced mushrooms. Fill the pre-cooked pie shape with parsnips, onion and mushrooms and almonds and sprinkle with cinnamon.

3. Whisk together the creamed mushrooms, cream cheese or quark and egg in a basin. Season with salt and pepper. Pour the mixture over the filling in the pie, sprinkle with the cheese and bake for about 25 minutes. Serve the pie warm with a crisp green salad

Giving nuts and almonds as a wedding gift is a common tradition in countries around the Mediterranean. In this custom, which dates from a long time ago, the nuts are symbols of secret sexual life and of fertility.

Broccoli quiche with walnuts

This also works well with cauliflower or both. You can roast the walnuts lightly in the oven, at 200°C, on a baking tray for about 10 minutes.

SERVES 6

My favourite pastry (see below)

Filling

About 500 g broccoli

125 g mozzarella cheese

2 eggs

200 g cream cheese

Grated rind of ½ lemon

1 clove of garlic

1 tsp thyme

Salt and pepper

100 – 150 g walnuts

1. Start by making the pastry and put it in the refrigerator. Set the oven to 225°C. Rinse the broccoli, slice the stalks fairly thinly and break the rest into florets. Blanch briefly in a little water.

2. Cut the mozzarella in slices. Whisk together the egg and cream cheese, season with lemon peel, garlic, thyme, salt and pepper.

3. Prick the quiche base with a fork and bake for 10 minutes. Lay the mozzarella in the bottom and then the broccoli. Pour the egg mix over. Place the walnuts evenly over the quiche. Bake for about 30 minutes or until the quiche has set and turned golden.

MY FAVOURITE PASTRY IN THE FOOD PROCESSOR

I have a favourite among pastry recipes, which is easy to work with. I use it both for sweet quiches and, as here, for savoury quiches. And you can vary the taste by adding nuts for example.

250 g flour

75 g butter

50 g cream cheese

1. Measure the flour into the processor. Add butter straight from the fridge, in cubes. Blend until the consistency is like coarse sand. Add the cream cheese and blend until the pastry sticks together.

2. Press the pastry into a loose-bottomed pie dish. Place in the refrigerator for 30 minutes. Set the oven to 200°C. Prick the base with a fork and bake blind for 10 minutes. Pour in the filling and bake in the bottom part of the oven for about 25 minutes.

Risotto with onions and Brazil nuts

SERVES 4

2 onions, finely chopped

20 cm leek, shredded

2 cloves garlic, finely chopped

Olive oil

300 g Arborio rice

200 ml white wine

800 ml water

1 vegetable stock cube

Salt and chilli pepper

2 tbsp butter

100 g grated Parmesan

100 g roasted Brazil nuts, coarsely chopped

1. Fry all the onion until soft, in olive oil in a big high-sided frying pan. Rinse the rice carefully and add it to the frying pan. Stir and allow to sizzle a little until the rice is glassy round the edges. Pour on the wine and leave to simmer gently until the wine is almost completely absorbed.

2. Meanwhile bring 800 ml water to the boil with the stock cube. Pour the stock over the rice in stages, as the rice absorbs the liquid. Stir frequently. Taste the rice. If it seems cooked and is beginning to become sticky, it is ready..

3. Season with salt and chilli pepper. Stir the butter and cheese into the risotto. Sprinkle with the nuts and serve.

Baked beetroot with roasted hazelnuts

Goat's cheese and tasty wholemeal bread taste wonderful with beetroot and with a crisp green salad makes a satisfying meal.

SERVES 3

6 beetroot

1 red onion

Dressing

3 tbsp balsamic vinegar

2 tbsp olive oil

1 tsp honey

Salt and pepper

50 g parsley, finely chopped

100 – 200 g hazelnuts, roasted, shelled and chopped

1. Set the oven to 200°C. Rinse the beetroot carefully but do not peel them and place them in a roasting dish. Bake in the oven for about an hour for winter beetroot and a little less for newly harvested small beet. Remove from the oven and allow to cool.

2. Peel and slice the beetroot, place in a bowl. Slice the red onion and add to the bowl. Mix the dressing and pour it over. Leave to stand and marinade at room temperature for a couple of hours. Sprinkle with masses of roasted hazelnuts just before you serve. Any leftovers can be kept for up to three days in the fridge.

Saffron cream with chilli and roasted macadamia nuts

100 g roasted macadamia nuts

100 ml mayonnaise (see basic recipe p. 88)

100 ml soured cream or crème fraîche

1 tsp paprika powder

½ packet saffron

Salt and chilli pepper

Grind the nuts fairly fine in the food processor. Mix together the mayonnaise and soured cream in a bowl and stir in the paprika powder, saffron, salt and chilli pepper and finally the ground nuts.

Pesto alla trapanese

SERVES 8

10 cloves of garlic

2 bunches of basil

50 g shelled and roasted sweet almonds

A few leaves of mint

6 tomatoes, skinned

3 tbsp olive oil

Use the mixer or food processor and blend the garlic, basil, almonds and mint to a fairly fine consistency. Add the tomatoes and oil, blend for a little longer.

Trapani is a harbour town on Sicily and it is almost as far west as one can go on the island. The influences of the nearby African continent are evident.

Romesco sauce with almonds

100 g blanched and peeled almonds

1 ripe tomato

2 roasted red peppers (see below)

1 tbsp red wine vinegar

3 cloves of garlic

Chilli pepper

Salt

50 ml fine olive oil

1. Roast the almonds in the oven for about 8 minutes or until they begin to snap, smell good and turn golden. Blend them in the food processor. Add the tomato, cut into small gateauxces, and the roasted peppers.

2. Add vinegar, garlic, chilli pepper and salt. Pour in the oil in a fine stream while the processor is running. This sauce keeps 3 to 4 days in the refrigerator.

ROASTED PEPPERS

Yellow and red peppers

Set the oven to 250°C and put the grill on. Cut the pepper into four gateauxces lengthwise, remove the seeds and any membranes. Lay the peppers on greaseproof paper on a baking tray with the skin uppermost and immediately place under the grill. When the pepper skins have begun to turn black they are ready. Remove from the oven, place in a plastic bag and tie it up. Leave them to cool in the bag. It will then be easy to remove the skin. The peppers have a wonderful flavour and are ready to use.

BASIC RECIPE FOR MAYONNAISE

All the ingredients should be at room temperature. If you have a mixer or food processor available, making mayonnaise is very easy. Otherwise it may help to decant some oil into a little jug with a spout for example. When you start whisking you have to drip the oil in one drop at a time. That is the secret of making a mayonnaise of the perfect consistency.

Mayonnaise in a mixer or food processor

2 egg yolks

1 tsp Dijon mustard

1 tbsp freshly squeezed lemon juice

200 -300 ml cold pressed rapeseed oil

Salt and pepper

1. Place the egg yolks, mustard and lemon juice in a mixer or food processor. Blend at a low speed for about 30 seconds.

2. Pour the oil in slowly in a thin stream. When the mayonnaise begins to thicken you can pour the oil in a little more quickly. Season with salt and pepper.

Mayonnaise by hand

Whisk together the egg yolks, mustard and lemon juice in a bowl. Pour the oil in a drop at a time until the mayonnaise begins to thicken and then continue with a thin stream of oil, whisking all the time. Season with salt and pepper.

Tip!   If you want a lower fat version, you can mix the mayonnaise with an equal quantity of soured cream or light crème fraîche.
You can also mix mayonnaise with a little water and ground nuts.

Walnut mayonnaise

2 egg yolks

200 ml rapeseed oil

50 walnuts, shelled

Pinch of chilli pepper

1 tsp grated lemon zest

Salt and pepper

Make sure all the ingredients are at room temperature. Place the egg yolks in a bowl, start by pouring the oil in a drop at a time whilst you whisk with an electric whisk. When the mayonnaise has begun to thicken, the oil may be poured in a thin stream until the whole lot is blended. Grind the nuts in a nut mill. Mix them into the mayonnaise together with the chilli pepper and the lemon zest. Season with salt and pepper.

Tip! You can also flavour the mayonnaise with other herbs, for example with dill and tarragon for fish, basil, tomato purée and chilli pepper for meat. Extra mustard is also nice and goes well with a lot of things.

"I went down into the garden of nuts to see the fruits of the valley, and to see whether the vine flourished, and the pomegranates budded."

Song of Solomon 6:10

Gremolata with walnuts or pecan nuts

A gremolata does not normally include nuts but this is a fantastic flavour enhancer to put on the table with grilled lamb, chicken, meat or fish.

100 g finely chopped roasted walnuts or pecan nuts

3 tbsp grated lemon zest

100 g parsley, finely chopped

1 tbsp garlic, finely chopped

Mix all the ingredients together and serve immediately. Any leftovers can be stored in a jar in the refrigerator for up to a week.

Hazelnut butter

50 g roasted hazelnuts, finely chopped

2 shallots, finely chopped and fried

1 tbsp Dijon mustard

Salt and pepper

100 g butter at room temperature

Mix the nuts, shallots and mustard. Season with salt and pepper. Beat into the butter with a fork. Wrap in cling film and shape into a roll. Place in the refrigerator. Cut into slices and serve with meat, fish or chicken for example.

Warm peanut sauce

There is a less sweet peanut butter in health food shops which I think is the best for this sauce.

About 300 ml water

50 g peanut butter

Juice of ½ lime

2 tbsp Japanese soy sauce

½ - 1 red chilli pepper, finely chopped

1 tsp honey

About 1 tbsp cornflour and a little water

Sea salt

Place everything except the cornflour in a saucepan and heat the ingredients while whisking them. Mix the cornflour and a little water and pour in, bring to the boil and simmer quickly until the sauce thickens. If you want a thicker sauce you can use a little more cornflour and water. Season with salt and serve immediately.

Petra's tasty dressing with hazelnuts

This is a real VIP among dressings and wonderful with a little cabbage and grated carrots or lightly cooked vegetables such as cauliflower and broccoli.

100 g roasted hazelnuts, chopped

100 ml single cream

1 tbsp cider vinegar

1 tbsp runny honey

Salt and pepper

Chopped cress

Just mix all the ingredients together and pour the dressing over the cold salad or the warm vegetables.

Tip! Try the hazelnut dressing on a salad of tasty mature cheese, parma ham and crisp lettuce leaves. A perfect little starter.

Picada

15 blanched, peeled and roasted almonds

15 roasted hazelnuts

100 g roasted pine nuts

1 slice stale wholemeal bread

3 cloves of garlic

5 stalks of parsley

Olive oil

Salt

1. Roast the almonds and nuts in the oven on greaseproof paper on a baking tray. Toast the bread under the grill or in the toaster and cut it into gateauxces. Place all the ingredients in a mixer or food processor. Blend to a fine-grained consistency, add the olive oil and blend to a reasonably thick paste.

2. The consistency should be fairly thick but you can dilute it with water if you want it thinner. Season with salt. Picada will keep in a jar with an airtight lid for up to a week in the fridge.

Salbitxada, hot Catalan sauce

100 g blanched, peeled and roasted sweet almonds

4 cloves of garlic

2 blanched tomatoes

1 tbsp chopped parsley

1 tbsp chopped chives

1 tbsp red vinegar

½ - 1 tsp chilli pepper

Olive oil

Blanch and roast the almonds on greaseproof paper on a baking tray for about 10 minutes. It's a good idea to use a handheld mixer, blender or food processor. First grind the almonds fairly finely. Add the garlic and blend a little more. Add the tomatoes, parsley, chives, vinegar, chilli and olive oil, a little at a time, and blend to a fairly smooth sauce.

Aubergine paté with hazelnuts

A fairly solid paté which tastes good with most things,
even on a buffet or as part of a tapas or meze meal.

2 aubergines
200 g hazelnuts
1 bunch parsley
2 cloves of garlic, crushed
1 tbsp lemon juice
50 ml olive oil
Salt and chilli pepper

1. Set the oven to 225°C. First place the aubergines in the centre of the oven for about 30 minutes. Then switch the grill on and transfer them to the grillpan and grill them until the outside is blackened. Turn them now and again. Turn off the grill.

2. Place the aubergines in a plastic bag and close it, leave to cool for a while.

3. Spread the nuts on greaseproof paper on a baking tray and roast them in the oven for about 10 minutes. Chop them finely in the food processor.

4. Peel the skin from the cooled aubergines and place the flesh in the food processor together with the parsley, garlic and lemon juice. Blend to a smooth paste. Pour in the oil, a little at a time, while the food processor is going. Season with salt and chilli.

Mixed spiced nuts for all kinds of uses

100 g walnuts
100 g Brazil nuts
100 g hazelnuts
1 tbsp ground coriander
1 tbsp ground ginger
1 tbsp paprika powder
1 tsp ground chilli pepper
Salt

1. Set the oven to 200°C. Start by roasting the coarsely chopped nuts on a baking tray in the oven for about 10 minutes.

2. Blend the nuts in a food processor or blender. Stir in all the spices. Store in a jar in the refrigerator. A delicious mixture of spices which goes well sprinkled on salads, in soup or on a slice of really tasty bread?

Avocado and mango paste with cashews

Absolutely great with grilled chicken and grilled pork but also with fish.

100 g chopped, salted and roasted cashew nuts

3 avocados

1 mango

2 cloves of garlic

1 tbsp mango balsamic vinegar or another balsamic vinegar

2 tbps lemon juice

1 tsp coriander

1 tsp ground cumin

Salt and pepper

Blend the nuts in the food processor. Cut the avocados in half and scoop out the flesh, peel and slice the mango and place all this in the food processor with the garlic, vinegar, lemon juice, coriander and cumin. Blend until not quite smooth, season with salt and pepper and serve.

Almond sauce with a flavour of the Middle East

Delicious with lamb in various guises.

50 g almonds

2 cloves of garlic

½ pot of fresh coriander

2 tsp paprika

2 tsp cumin

100 ml olive oil

Juice of 1 lime

Salt and chilli pepper

1. Blend the almonds, garlic, coriander, paprika and cumin in a food processor or blender, to a smooth sauce. Pour the oil in slowly in a thin stream.

2. Add the lime juice, season with salt and chilli.

Five kinds of pesto

PESTO GENOVESE

This is the original, with pine nuts, basil, parmesan and olive oil. The other pesto mixtures are made in the same way.

4 cloves of garlic

50 g pine nuts

2 jars of fresh basil

Sea salt flakes

50 g grated parmesan

100 – 150 ml virgin olive oil

1. Peel the garlic and place with the pine nuts, basil and salt in a food processor and blend until the mixture is quite fine.

2. Add the cheese and oil in turns and blend to a creamy consistency similar to mayonnaise.

PESTO WITH HAZELNUTS

50 g hazelnuts

1 bunch of parsley

50 g strong cheese, grated

150 ml rapeseed oil

Salt and pepper

PESTO WITH WALNUTS

2 cloves of garlic

50 g walnuts

50 g rocket

50 g grated Swedish Grevé cheese (slightly sweet and tasting of curds) or similar

Salt and chilli pepper

100 – 150 ml rapeseed or sunflower oil

PESTO WITH PISTACHIO NUTS

1 clove of garlic

50 g pistachio nuts

1 bunch dill

50 g grated Herrgård (mild) cheese or similar

Grated rind of ½ lemon

Lemon juice

150 ml rapeseed or sunflower oil

Salt and pepper

Follow the recipe for Pesto Genovese. Chop the dill separately and stir it in by hand at the end. That makes a more attractive-looking, less soggy pesto and the dill flavour is stronger.

PESTO FOR AN EMPTY PURSE WITH TREASURES FROM THE LARDER

Peanuts
Any herbs
Mixed leftover cheese
Whatever oil you have
Salt and pepper

Tapenade with green olives and cashew nuts

50 g salted and roasted cashew nuts
25 – 30 green olives with lemon
2 cloves of garlic
Juice of ½ lemon

First blend the nuts in the food processor or blender. Add the olives and garlic and blend to a firm consistency. Add the oil a little at a time and finally the lemon juice.

Hazelnut grapes

The perfect little nibble to have with an aperitif, for a gathering or whenever you feel like it!

200 g hazelnuts
100 ml mascarpone
100 g mild gorgonzola
About 200 g green and/or black grapes

1. Set the oven to 200°C. Roast the nuts for about 8 minutes on a baking tray in the oven, or until they are golden. If you rub the nuts a little in a tea towel you will get rid of most of the skin. Chop them fairly small and place on a plate.

2. Mix the mascarpone and gorgonzola. Rinse and drain the grapes.

3. It's a little tricky to get the cheese to stick all over the grapes. If you have the cheese cream on a plate, you can place a few grapes at a time on top and turn them over with a spoon. The cheese will not cover them completely but that doesn't matter. Then roll them in the chopped nuts. Even if they don't look perfect, they taste wonderful.

Avocado au gratin with nuts and parma ham

SERVES 4

2 large avocados

2 stems of celery

100 g parma ham

50 g walnuts

100 g creamy mild white or blue veined cheese

1. Set the oven to 250°C. Split the avocados and remove the stones. Place the halves on individual ovenproof dishes. Cut the celery and ham into small strips, chop the nuts roughly and mix these three ingredients together.

2. Fill the avocado halves with the mix. Cut the cheese into four gateauxces. Place each gateauxce on top of a filled avocado. Grill for 5 minutes or until the cheese has begun to melt and turn slightly brown. Eat immediately!

Bruschetta with pine nuts

A few slices of a good bread

Olive oil

Garlic

Mozzarella, sliced

Tomatoes, sliced

Salt and pepper

Pine nuts

Basil

1. Set the oven to 200°C. Sprinkle a little oil over the slices of bread and toast them on a baking tray covered with greaseproof paper. Take out the bread and rub it with a cut clove of garlic.

2. Place a slice of mozzarella, a slice of tomato, salt, pepper and pine nuts on each slice of bread and decorate with fresh basil.

Hazelnut roulade with mulled pears

This recipe was inspired by Markus Aujalay, Swedish Chef of the Year 2004.

4 small or 2 large pears

500 ml mulled wine

1 stick of cinnamon

Cheese roll

300 g blue cheese

100 ml cream cheese

200 g chopped roasted hazelnuts

A few stems of celery

1. Cut the celery into narrow strips, about 10 cm long. Place the strips in a glass of water in the fridge. The strips will curl into fantastic shapes after a few hours and will look great when served.

2. Peel and cook the pears in the mulled wine with the cinnamon stick until they are soft.

3. Mash the blue cheese with the cream cheese, it's easiest with a fork. Place in the fridge.

4. Set the oven to 200°C. Roast the nuts on greaseproof paper on a baking tray for about 10 minutes. Rub the skins off with a tea towel as far as you can. Chop the nuts.

5. Take out the cheese mix, tip it on to a gateauxce of cling film, wrap it up and form into a roll. Place the chopped nuts on a dish, unwrap the cheese roll on top of them and roll it until it is covered with nuts. Wrap it in a fresh gateauxce of cling film until it is time to serve it.

6. Place one pear or pear half on each plate, cut the cheese roll in slices and place one or two slices next to the pear and garnish with the celery.

Cheesy nuts

Small tasty cheesy nuts to serve with a bowl of smooth artichoke soup or a spicy tomato soup for example.

MAKES 40 CHEESY NUTS

100 g butter

50 g walnuts

150 g parmesan cheese in small gateauxces

200 g plain flour

100 g wholemeal flour

½ tsp baking powder

1 tbsp water

2 – 4 tbsp whole or chopped walnuts to garnish

1. Cut the butter into small gateauxces. Blend the nuts roughly in a food processor. Add the parmesan cheese and blend until the cheese is like fine breadcrumbs. Add the other ingredients and blend to a dough.

2. Roll out the dough in two lengths. Leave them to go hard in the fridge for about 1 hour. Set the oven to 200°C. Cut the roll in gateauxces and press half a walnut into each or dip one cut side into chopped nuts. Place them on greaseproof paper on a baking tray in the oven. Bake in the centre of the oven for about 10 – 12 minutes.

In many folk tales nuts symbolise something mysterious. The hard shell, which is difficult to crack, hides something valuable which someone wants to get hold of.

Cones with hazelnut ice cream and chocolate toppings

A great December dessert which can of course be served at any time of year.

4 - 8 CONES DEPENDING ON THEIR SIZE
½ litre (or more) good vanilla ice cream
100 g roasted hazelnuts, chopped

Plastic pockets and tape

Dark chocolate
Pastry cutters

1. Cut out circles from the plastic pockets and tape them into cone shapes.

2. Roast the hazelnuts in the oven at 200°C for about 10 minutes.

3. Thaw the ice cream a little, place in a bowl and mix with the hazelnuts. Fill the cones with the ice cream. Place them in a rectangular baking tin for example, which you have first filled with dried peas or beans, so that the cones can stand up. Place in the freezer overnight or for at least 4 hours.

4. Place greaseproof paper on a baking tray and lay the pastry cutters on top. Melt the chocolate over a pan of hot water and pour a thin layer of chocolate into the shapes, leave to harden.

5. Remove the plastic from the cones and place them upside down on a dish, place a cocktail stick in the top. Remove the chocolate shapes from their cutters and hook them on to cocktail sticks on top of the cones. Serve with segments of mandarin or orange (see page 106).

Sweet eggy bread with nuts

A delicious winter dessert after a light meal such as soup.

SERVES 4

1 egg
200 ml milk
4 slices wholemeal bread
Butter

200 ml custard (whichever kind you like best)

100 g prunes, without stones
200 ml freshly squeezed orange juice
100 g caster sugar
50 g coarsely chopped walnuts

1. Whisk the egg and milk in a bowl, dip the slices of bread in the mixture and fry the bread in butter in a frying pan. Take out and place on greaseproof paper to drain the fat.

2. Make your favourite custard.

3. Cook the prunes, orange juice and sugar until they reach a syrupy consistency, add the nuts. Place a slice of bread in the middle of the plate, add a scoop of custard and decorate with prunes and nuts and add the syrup as sauce.

Calvados baked apples in marzipan

An adult dessert for the season when the leaves are starting to fall and there is a glut of apples. Try a little spoonful of lightly whipped cream with it, heavenly!
Use cooking apples, they taste best.

SERVES 4

2 fairly large apples
75 g readymade marzipan (or see page 135)
1 egg
2 tbsp + 2 tbsp Calvados
50 g flaked almonds

1. Set the oven to 200°C. Peel, halve across and core the apples. Simmer them gently in water for a couple of minutes.

2. Grease four individual ovenproof dishes or use one big dish for the whole dessert.

3. Blend the marzipan, egg and 2 tbsp Calvados in a food processor.

4. Divide the mix between the dishes or pour into one big dish, press the apples into it with the round side down, pour Calvados into the holes where the core was and sprinkle with flaked almonds. Place in the oven for about 10 minutes or until the marzipan and flaked almonds have begun to turn brown.

Walnut ice with black dates

A fun, tasty and different dessert which perhaps suits the winter best. If you have an ice cream maker and want to make the walnut ice cream yourself, there is a recipe on page 106.

SERVES 4

400 g dates
500 ml strong coffee
1 tbsp sugar
1 tsp ground cardamom

Vanilla ice cream
100 g walnuts

1. Take the stones out of the dates and place the dates in a bowl. Pour the prepared coffee into a saucepan, heat through and allow the sugar to melt in it. Add the cardamom. Pour half the coffee over the dates and leave to stand in the refrigerator for at least 8 hours.

2. Roast the walnuts on a baking tray in the oven at 200°C for about 10 minutes. Leave to cool and chop the nuts roughly. Take the ice cream from the freezer, allow to soften a little, mix with the nuts and return to the freezer. Serve the dates and ice cream with the remaining coffee in bowls

Pliny was a Roman official who lived almost two thousand years ago. He believed that the shadow of the walnut tree was harmful. If you look beneath a walnut tree you will see that nothing grows there and this is why the walnut tree became a symbol of selfishness.

A great little pudding

A dessert for those with nut allergy.
It contains coconut and pine nuts but none of
the nuts which allergy sufferers usually react
to. It's just the right end to a rich dinner
when you fancy something sweet but small.

SERVES 4 – 6

50 g pudding rice

200 ml water

½ stick of vanilla

50 g coconut flakes

300 ml coconut milk

100 g caster sugar

50 g pine nuts

Fresh pineapple

1 tbsp butter

1 tbsp sugar

Small jelly moulds or other moulds

1. Boil the rice and water with the vanilla and
   coconut flakes for 10 minutes. Pour in the
   coconut milk a little at a time and boil until
   it forms a firm pasty consistency. Place to
   one side.

2. Peel the pineapple and cut it in slices. Cut
   one slice into small pieces which will fit in
   the bottom of the moulds.

3. Brush the moulds with a little neutral
   cooking oil. Melt the butter and sugar in a
   saucepan. Divide the pineapple pieces
   between the moulds, distribute the butter
   and sugar mix over the fruit.

4. Bring the rice pudding mix to the boil again
   and mix in the sugar, simmer for a minute or
   two and add the pine nuts. Share out the rice
   between the moulds and chill. Turn out the
   moulds on plates when you are ready to
   serve up, sprinkle a few extra pine nuts over
   them and garnish with pineapple slices.

Walnut ice

200 ml milk
200 ml yoghurt
100 ml runny honey
1 tsp vanilla sugar
75 g roasted walnuts, roughly chopped

Mix the milk, yoghurt, honey and vanilla sugar in a bowl. Set the ice cream maker going and pour in the mix, alternating with walnuts, whilst the machine is running. It takes about 45 minutes until the ice cream is ready, depending on how cold the ingredients are.

Tip! You need an ice cream maker for this dessert. But you can also buy good vanilla ice cream, allow it to melt a little, then mix in the walnuts and re-freeze.

In the story of Thumbelina by Hans Christian Andersen, Thumbelina lay sleeping in a walnut shell. Her mother and father couldn't have children but they got a seed from a witch which grew up into a flower. In the flower sat little Thumbelina. "A finely polished walnut shell formed her cradle, and therein, on a bed of violets, under a rose-leaf coverlet, slept Thumbelina."

Lemon pannacotta with pistachio nuts

SERVES 4

Grated rind of 1 lemon
400 ml single cream
150 g jam-making sugar*

Segments cut from 1 lime (see below)
50 g finely chopped pistachio nuts
Strawberries

1. Rinse the lime carefully and grate the rind. Simmer the cream and lemon peel over a low heat. Stir in the sugar, bring to the boil and leave to simmer for a couple of minutes. Pour into individual moulds or ramekins. Place in the fridge.

2. Chop the nuts finely. Turn out the pannacotta on to dishes, sprinkle with the chopped nuts and garnish with lime segments and strawberries.

CITRUS FRUIT IN SMALL SEGMENTS

1. Peel the fruit with a sharp knife and make sure you get rid of all the white pith.

2. Cut out the segments between the membranes.

3. Ready to serve.

Hazelnut meringues

The first time I tasted hazelnut meringues was in a 'pasticceria' in Taormina on Sicily.
What fantastic meringues! I don't have that precise recipe but this is the closest I can get.

400 g hazelnuts
250 g icing sugar
3 egg whites
A pinch of salt

1. Set the oven to 175°C. Roast the hazelnuts in the oven for 10 – 15 minutes. Tip the nuts into a tea towel and rub away as much of the skin as you can. Chop the nuts fairly small.

2. Sieve the icing sugar carefully into a bowl to get rid of any lumps.

3. Whisk the egg whites with a little salt in a clean bowl. It's best to use an electric whisk. Whisk until the whites are frothy.

4. Add the icing sugar, a little at a time, and whisk until the mixture forms peaks. The egg should stick to the bowl if you turn it upside down.

5. Stir the chopped hazelnuts carefully into the mixture and drop spoonfuls of the mixture on to one or two baking trays covered with greaseproof paper. If you use a tablespoon the meringues will be the right size. The spoonfuls spread quite a bit so leave about 6 – 8 cm between them. Bake in the centre of the oven for 25 – 30 minutes.

6. Drag the paper with the meringues on to a rack and leave to cool. Store in airtight tins in a dark dry place.

Figs in rum with roasted pecan nuts

With the help of two saucepans and a 100 ml measure, this dessert is easy to make.

SERVES 4

200 ml vanilla yoghurt

100 ml matured dark rum
100 ml water
200 g caster sugar
8 fresh figs

100 g roasted pecan nuts

1. Pour the vanilla yoghurt into a bowl and stand it in the freezer.

2. Bring the rum, water and sugar to the boil in a saucepan. Place the figs in another saucepan, pour the rum mix over, bring to the boil and simmer for 15 – 20 minutes.

3. Strain the liquor into the first saucepan and boil until reduced by about half. Pour the hot liquor over the figs and leave to cool. Serve the figs with the vanilla yoghurt ice cream and sprinkle with the roasted pecan nuts.

Since hazelnuts have been around for such a long time in mankind's history, they appear in various mythical contexts. Hazel trees had already spread quite widely by 7500 – 5000 B.C. and were the most dominant vegetation on the British Isles and in Scandinavia. So it's not surprising that they came to play a part in Celtic and Scandinavian mythology. Many religious ceremonies among the Celts and Druids were held in hazel groves.

The hazel protects against the lightning of Thor, god of thunder, according to Scandinavian mythology. In Swedish folklore the hazel played its part as a divining rod and in various rites, associated among other things with the magical Midsummer's Night. You could also tell the future from hazelnuts on Halloween, which was originally a heathen festival. Halloween was also called 'nutcracker' night.

Tarte with pecan and macadamia nuts

Are you having a party in the early summer in the middle of the day for a graduation, confirmation, wedding or birthday? If so a cold buffet is usually a good idea and you can make much of a few nice sweets to serve with the coffee. This tarte can be made several days beforehand and if there are nut allergy sufferers among your guests, you can replace the nuts with pine nuts and keep the coconut. If you are also making hazelnut cake (see page 111) you will find a use for both the egg whites and the yolks.

1 batch pastry with cream cheese (see page 83)

100 g macadamia nuts

100 g pecan nuts

100 g desiccated coconut

25 g butter

100 g light brown sugar

4 egg yolks

100 ml coconut milk

Grated rind of 1 lemon

1. Set the oven to 175°C. Use a loose-bottomed pie dish. Line the dish with the pastry, prick the bottom with a fork. Chill for at least 15 minutes. Bake the pie blind for about 15 minutes. Leave to cool.

2. Place the nuts on a baking tray and roast for about 5 minutes in the oven, or until they have begun to turn brown. You may also toast the desiccated coconut in a big frying pan, to bring out the flavour even more.

3. Melt the butter in a saucepan, stir in the sugar and remove the pan from the heat when the sugar has melted.

4. Whisk the egg yolks and coconut milk together in a bowl, whisk in the butter and sugar mixture. Spread the nuts and coconut over the pastry shell, sprinkle on the lime peel, pour the egg mixture over and bake in the centre of the oven for about 20 minutes.

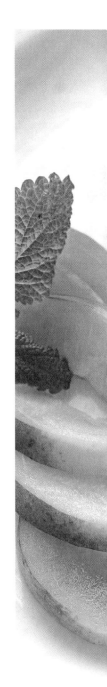

Tasty hazelnut cake

A delicious cake with a strong flavour of hazelnuts. It's a good idea to serve it with strong coffee and a sweet dessert wine. You could call this a low-fat cake: no cooking fat and no egg yolks. See picture on page 129.

300 g hazelnuts
300 g sugar
2 tsp vanilla sugar
100 g self raising flour
6 egg whites
Pinch salt

Icing sugar

1. Set the oven to 175°C. Grease a round loose-bottomed cake tin, about 22 cm in diameter, and sprinkle with breadcrumbs.

2. Chop the nuts in the food processor, mix in half the sugar, vanilla sugar and flour. Remove the blades and use the food processor as a bowl to mix the cake in.

3. Whisk the egg whites with a pinch of salt using an electric whisk. Add the remaining sugar, a little at a time, and whisk for 3 – 4 minutes until the mixture stands in peaks.

4. Fold the egg whites carefully into the nut mixture, spread the mixture over the tin and bake for about 1 hour. Leave to cool and remove from the tin, sprinkle with a little icing sugar before serving.

Chocolate and pistachio cake with raspberries and Baileys

Many years ago I was in Paris one autumn with my daughter. We used to eat dinner in a little place near the hotel and one evening they served up an unforgettable tarte for dessert. I have experimented and although I can't claim that it was exactly like this, it is almost the same and at least equally nice.

200 g bought marzipan (or see page 135)
100 g pistachio nuts, finely chopped
1 egg

Chocolate cream

400 ml single cream

1 tbsp cocoa

2 tbsp strong coffee or espresso

100 g dark chocolate with about 70% cocoa content

100 g preserving sugar

Baileys to serve, if liked
Raspberries

1. Set the oven to 175°C. Pull the marzipan apart and mix with the chopped nuts and egg. You can do all this in a food processor. Grease a round loose-bottomed pie dish. Tip the mixture in and bake for 15 minutes. Remove from the oven and allow to cool.

2. Simmer the cream, cocoa and coffee over a low heat. Melt the chocolate over a pan of boiling water and mix with the hot cream.

Stir in the sugar, bring to the boil and simmer for a few minutes, then remove the saucepan from the heat. Leave to cool a little until the chocolate mix begins to thicken.

3. Pour the chocolate mix over the cold almond base, leave to chill until the chocolate has set. Remove the tarte from the tin and cut into small slices. If you like, pour a little Baileys into a serving dish, place the pieces of tarte on this and garnish with raspberries.

Apple cake with nuts and lemon

My daughter taught me how to make this apple cake when she was about nine. They'd made it at school and she was so proud that she could make apple cake. It's still the apple cake we make most often in our family because it is so easy. Here I've taken it slightly more upmarket by adding almonds and raisins.

SERVES 4 – 6

6 cooking apples

125 g butter

150 g oats

50 g sugar

100 g chopped almonds

50 g raisins

Grated rind of 1 lemon

1. Set the oven to 225°C. Core the apples and cut them into small pieces. Place them in a greased cake tin.

2. Melt the butter in a saucepan, add the oats, sugar, almonds and raisins.

3. Sprinkle the lemon peel over the apples, pour the oat mixture over and bake in the oven for about 30 minutes.

Almond macaroons

A macaroon with more almonds than usual and a great flavour.

50 g almonds

150 g bought marzipan (or see page 135 for the recipe)

1 – 2 egg whites

Filling

100 g butter

1 tbsp vanilla sugar

2 tbsp icing sugar

1 tbsp cocoa

Coating

200 g dark chocolate, min. 70% cocoa content

1 – 2 tbsp neutral cooking oil

1. Set the oven to 175°C. Line a baking tray with greaseproof paper. Mince the almonds in the food processor. Knead the marzipan roughly and mix with one egg white in the food processor. If it looks very hard and dry you can add another egg white.

2. Place one tablespoonful of mixture for each macaroon on the baking tray. Bake for 8 – 10 minutes. Leave the biscuits to cool on the paper on a rack.

3. Mix together at room temperature the butter, vanilla sugar, icing sugar and cocoa. Spread the filling on the flat underside of the biscuits. Place in the fridge for at least 15 minutes.

4. Melt the chocolate in a bowl over a pan of boiling water, mix with the oil and spread over the filling on the biscuits. Or dip the biscuits in the chocolate. Place in a cool place until the chocolate has set.

The Impressionists and Expressionists who lived in the nineteenth century also painted still life pictures with nuts. Eduard Manet, Pierre-Auguste Renoir, Henri Fantin-Latour and William Harnett painted fine still life pictures which included almonds, and not least Harnett painted an exquisite still life in 1876 with shelled almonds, apples, a few grapes and a glass of wine.

Walnut gateau

This moderately sweet and relatively low fat gateau could become your favourite. Adding the cream afterwards is mainly because it's easier to squirt it on but of course you could leave it out altogether.

5 eggs
200 g sugar
100 g walnuts
100 g flour
2 tbsp cocoa
1 tsp vanilla sugar
1 tsp baking powder

Filling
100 g walnuts
200 ml ricotta
6 – 8 canned or
cooked pear halves

About 20 good big walnuts
150 ml whipping cream
200 ml ricotta

1. Set the oven to 175°C. Grease a round tin and sprinkle with breadcrumbs. Whisk the eggs and sugar to a froth with an electric whisk.

2. Blend 100 g walnuts in a blender or chop them fairly small by hand. Mix with the flour, cocoa, vanilla sugar and baking powder. Fold the mixture into the beaten egg whites.

3. Bake the cake for 35 – 40 minutes, leave to cool and turn out.

4. Roast the nuts for the filling on a baking tray in the oven until they have begun to brown and a delicious aroma is filling the air. Take care, because they don't take long, about 10 minutes.

5. Set aside the nuts for decoration and chop the remainder roughly.

6. Divide the cake into three layers and place one on an attractive serving dish. Mix the chopped walnuts with the ricotta. Chop the pears fairly small.

7. Divide the chopped pears and walnut ricotta between the layers. Whisk the cream fairly stiff and mix with the ricotta, spread about half the mixture over the whole gateau. Squirt a pattern of cream on or just spread the rest of the cream over it, decorate with the whole walnuts. Serve canned or cooked pears with the gateau if liked.

Camille Pissaro must have liked walnut trees, because he has masses of paintings of just such trees. Vincent van Gogh and Claude Monet each painted several pictures of pine trees.

Spice cake with hazelnut butter and saffron cream

A really delicious little Christmas confection which tastes great with mulled wine.

Roulade

3 eggs

150 g sugar

200 g flour

2 tbsp cocoa

2 tsp ground cinnamon

2 tsp ground ginger

1 tsp vanilla sugar

1 tsp baking powder

1 tbsp caster sugar

Filling

About 200 g hazelnut butter (see page 119)

To decorate

100 ml whipping cream

½ g saffron

100 ml cream cheese

100 g chopped roasted hazelnuts

1. Set the oven to 250°C and line a baking tray or roasting dish with greaseproof paper. Place another piece of greaseproof paper on the worktop and sprinkle about 1 tbsp sugar on it. Take out the hazelnut butter and place the container in a bowl of warm water so that it softens and is easier to spread on the roulade.

2. Whisk the eggs and sugar to a foam in a bowl, using an electric whisk.

3. Mix the flour, spices, vanilla sugar and baking powder well in a smaller bowl.

4. Fold the flour mixture into the beaten eggs and stir. Pour out and spread the mixture over the baking tray or roasting dish using a spatula. Bake in the centre of the oven for about 5 minutes.

5. Remove from the oven and turn out the roulade on the sugared greaseproof paper. Spread carefully with hazelnut butter. You can drop spoonfuls on first so that it melts a little on the warm surface and then spread it. Roll the roulade up and leave it to cool.

6. Whip the cream. Mix the saffron with the cream cheese and stir this into the whipped cream. Cut the roulade into slices and squirt or spoon the cream on to the slices. Sprinkle with the roasted nuts and serve – it's nice with mulled wine!

Hazelnut butter

Delicious as a filling in cakes and gateaux or with pancakes or crêpes.

200 g hazelnuts
400 ml ricotta
2 tsp vanilla sugar
2 tbsp confectioner's sugar

1. Roast the hazelnuts on a tray in the oven at 200°C until they begin to brown. Leave to cool and chop them in the blender.

2. Heat half of the ricotta in a saucepan, stir in the confectioner's sugar and simmer for 30 seconds. Mix in the nuts, the rest of the ricotta and flavour with the vanilla sugar. When the butter has cooled it should be quite hard. Leave it to stand at room temperature before you want to serve it. If you spoon it on to a hot cake it's easier to spread.

Fruit and nut bread

Serve the bread with mature cheese or green-veined cheese.

2 LOAVES

1 litre yoghurt

200 ml treacle

1 tbsp sea salt

1 tsp ground cumin

1 kg sifted rye flour

4 tsp bicarbonate of soda

2 tsp baking powder

300 g pistachios

100 g dried apricots

100 g slices of dried apple

1. Set the oven to 100°C. Mix together the yoghurt, treacle, salt and cumin. Mix the rye flour, bicarbonate and baking powder separately and stir into the yoghurt mix, a little at a time, until there is an even, but still sticky, dough.

2. Roast the nuts in a dry frying pan. Tip them on to a tea towel and rub off the skin. Dice the apricots and apples. Stir everything into the dough.

3. Divide the dough into two halves. Grease two long bread tins and lay the dough in them. Smooth the surface with a little flour on your hands.

4. Bake the bread in the bottom of the oven for about 1 hour. Raise the temperature to 150 degrees and bake for a further 45 minutes. Turn off the heat and allow the bread to stand in the residual heat for about 20 minutes. Turn it out on to a rack. Leave to cool under a cloth.

Bread, buns and rusks

Walnut bread

500 ml water
10 g yeast
2 tsp sea salt
2 tbsp olive oil
1100 – 1200 g spelt flour
100 g coarsely chopped walnuts

1. Boil the water. Crumble the yeast in a bowl and pour the water over to dissolve the yeast. Add the salt and oil.

2. Work the flour in, alternating with the walnuts, working the latter in by hand. The dough should be fairly loose. Leave to prove at room temperature for about 2 hours. Set the oven to 250°C.

3. Flour a baking tray. Turn out the dough on a chopping board, divide in half with a knife without kneading it first. Twist each half gently as you would wring out a wet garment but more carefully. Lay the loaves on the tray and sprinkle a little flour over them.

4. Bake the bread for 10 minutes at 250°C, then reduce the heat to 150°C and bake for another 20 minutes. Leave the bread to cool under a cloth.

Focaccia with almonds and cherry tomatoes

A lovely bread to offer at the table with soup or perhaps just with a glass of wine and a little cheese.

½ packet of yeast (25 g)
250 ml water
50 ml olive oil
1 tsp sea salt
300 g flour
300 g durum wheat

About 10 cherry tomatoes
Almonds
Rosemary
Olive oil
Sea salt

1. Crumble the yeast into a bowl. Boil the water and pour over the yeast. Stir and add the oil and salt. Work in turns, knead thoroughly. Leave to prove for 30 minutes. Set the oven to 225°C. Oil a roasting dish or similar and press out the dough, which should be about 2.5cm thick.

2. Press the tomatoes on to the dough at regular intervals, do the same with the almonds and poke sprigs of rosemary in here and there. Sprinkle with a little olive oil and salt flakes. Bake for 15 minutes.

A typical Christmas game involving nuts is 'Filipin'. When someone cracks a nut that has two kernels he or she can challenge somebody to play Filipin. The game is to bet that the one who forgets to say Filipin next time they meet will owe the other one a meal, a car wash, a cinema ticket or something like that. It's usually almonds that have two kernels but it might also involve another type of nut, which normally contains one but in some cases may have two.

Pistachio muffins

These delicious cookies are shown in the picture on page 129..

20 MEDIUM-SIZED, 8 LARGE
OR 35 – 40 SMALL

100 g pistachio nuts

100 g butter or margarine

2 eggs

300 g sugar

100 g potato flour

100 g wheat flour

1 tsp baking powder

Grated rind of 1 lime

100 ml milk

1. Set the oven to 200°C. Place cake cases (whichever size you choose) on a baking tray. Grind the pistachios in a nut grinder. Melt the butter and leave to cool.

2. Whisk the eggs and sugar until light and fluffy. Mix together the potato flour, plain flour, baking powder, lime peel and ground nuts in a bowl. Stir the flour mix alternating with the milk and butter into the beaten eggs. Divide the mixture between the cake cases and bake in the centre of the oven for 10 – 15 minutes depending on the size.

In both Greek and Roman mythology the walnut tree was the tree of the god Jupiter. The original name 'Jovis glans' means Jove's acorns. It is also a symbol of fertility for the Greek goddess Artemis and the Roman goddess Diana. At religious festivals and weddings in Rome nuts were a common feature, since they were considered food for the gods.

Nut rusks

In Italy you are given crunchy rusks (cantucci) with a glass of 'vin santo'. They are usually baked with sweet almonds but I like the taste of hazelnuts so much that I use them instead.

ABOUT 16 LARGE OR 25 SMALLER RUSKS

200 g hazelnuts

75 g butter

350 g caster sugar

3 eggs

600 – 700 g flour

1 tsp baking powder

1 tbsp vanilla sugar

Finely grated rind of 1 orange

1. Set oven to 200°C. Roast the nuts on a baking tray in the oven for 10 minutes. Tip them into a tea towel and rub off most of the skins. Chop the nuts coarsely.

2. Mix together the butter and sugar, it's easiest with an electric whisk, then beat in the eggs, one at a time.

3. Mix the flour, baking powder, vanilla sugar, chopped nuts and orange peel in a bowl separately. Mix this mixture into the other mixture and stir to form a dough.

4. Divide the dough into four, form lengths and lay them on greaseproof paper on a baking

tray. Bake for 20 minutes in the centre of the oven. Remove from the oven and reduce the heat to 100°C.

5. Cut the lengths directly on the baking tray in diagonal pieces and dry them out slowly for almost an hour in the oven. When they are done they should be completely dry.

Almond buns

ABOUT 20 BUNS

8 bitter almonds

100 g sugar

75 g butter

1 egg

150 ml soured milk
(or runny yoghurt)

2 tsp baking powder

400 – 450 g self-raising flour

Chopped sweet almonds

1. Set the oven to 225°C. Line two baking trays with greaseproof paper. Grind the almonds in a nut grinder. Mix together the sugar and butter until soft and fluffy and almost white. Add the egg, soured milk, hartshorn, almonds and flour.

2. Make the dough into a roll and cut into about 20 pieces. Lay the pieces on the baking trays and form into small rolls, sprinkle with the chopped almonds. Bake for about 10 minutes. Leave to cool on a wire rack. Store in a tin with a lid on in a dry place.

Warning!   Bitter almonds in large quantities are not good for you, they can even be poisonous. Where the almond tree grows, for example on Sicily, they say that these trees are like love: bitter and sweet. The bitter and sweet almonds actually grow on the same tree. The bitter almond can only be distinguished when the tree is flowering, as the flowers of the bitter almond are pink and red, the redder they are the more bitter. But most of the flowers are a beautiful white.

The queen of detective novel writers, Agatha Christie, was a nurse and worked in the hospital pharmacy during the First World War. Her knowledge of medicine and poisons therefore came in very useful when she started to write detective stories. In 'Sparkling Cyanide', which was published in 1944, she uses a substance which is found among other things in bitter almonds and can form potassium cyanide in a chemical compound. The action of the book revolves around the rich Rose Mary Barton who drops dead after a glass of champagne and everything suggests that she has committed suicide. But there is an embittered sister who was cheated of her inheritance, a number of disappointed lovers and mysterious letters which suggest that the truth lies elsewhere...

Nut medallions

You can choose your own combination of nuts and raisins but it looks good if there are several different shapes and colours on each medallion. This makes an elegant confection which you can place in a small box and give away as a present.

ABOUT 20 MEDALLIONS

20 pieces of dark chocolate

Whole walnuts

Pistachio nuts

Sweet almonds

Hazelnuts

Raisins

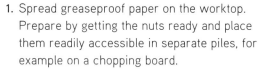

1. Spread greaseproof paper on the worktop. Prepare by getting the nuts ready and place them readily accessible in separate piles, for example on a chopping board.

2. Melt the chocolate over a saucepan of hot water and spoon five little heaps at a time on to the greaseproof paper. Using the nuts and raisins, flatten the medallions out. Leave to cool and set.

Coconut balls

You can call these coconut balls a quick-to-make sweet. They are soft in consistency which means they're a bit difficult to bite into, so it's best to roll small balls and enjoy them whole. Delicious!

200 ml ricotta

1 tsp vanilla sugar

1 – 2 tbsp lemon-flavoured confectioner's sugar or icing sugar

Grated peel of 1 organic lemon

100 – 200 g desiccated coconut

Mix the ricotta with the vanilla sugar and icing sugar, lemon peel and 1 tbsp coconut. Place spoonfuls of the mixture on a dish full of desiccated coconut and roll them around carefully till they form small round balls which are completely covered with coconut. Arrange them on a dish with a little coconut in the bottom.

Peanut bananas

Small, moderately healthy, light bites.

200 g chopped roasted peanuts, salted or unsalted

3 bananas

100 g dark chocolate

1. Spread out a piece of greaseproof paper and lay the chopped peanuts on it. Peel and slice the bananas in pieces between 2-3 cm thick.

2. Melt the chocolate over a pan of hot water, take one piece of banana at a time, using a cocktail stick and dip in the chocolate, roll immediately in the peanuts and place on another piece of greaseproof paper to set.

Panforte with hazelnuts

This sweet from Tuscany is deliciously crunchy with a lovely aroma of Christmas. The city of Siena is famous for its sweets and you can find panforte in all the confectioners shops in Siena throughout the year. The recipe is supposed to be at least a thousand years old. The cake is quick to make but you have to be alert to the critical moment when the mixture needs to be poured into the mould.

200 g hazelnuts

1 tsp ground coriander

1 tsp ground cinnamon

1 tsp ground cloves

1 tsp ground nutmeg

1 tsp freshly ground black pepper

Grated rind of 2 well washed organic oranges

Grated rind of 2 well washed organic lemons

100 g flour

1 tbsp cocoa (may be omitted)

150 g sugar

4 tbsp honey

2 tbsp buter

Icing sugar

1. Since the cake has a consistency reminiscent of toffee, it is important to take care how you prepare the tin. So take your time with the preparation because in the end that will help you. See the tip below.

2. Set the oven to 150°C, spread the nuts on a baking tray and roast them for 6 – 10 minutes. Tip them on to a tea towel and rub them so that most of the skin comes off. Remove the nuts and place in a bowl. Mix in all the spices, the lemon peel and flour and stir. If you would like a slightly darker colour in your cake you can add a little cocoa.

3. Melt the sugar and honey together slowly in a high-sided saucepan. Bring to the boil and allow to simmer fairly fast for about 1 minute. Add the butter in dabs and mix rapidly.

4. Now you need to be really quick. Pour the nut and spice mixture directly into the saucepan, mix quickly. If the mixture cools it sets and becomes impossible to handle. You can heat it over a pan of hot water if the worst comes to the worst.

5. Pour the mixture into the tin but don't bother to spread it, it does that itself in the heat of the oven. Bake at 150°C for about 15 minutes. Leave the cake to cool before removing it from the tin. It can be a good idea to bang the tin on the table first. Remove the greaseproof paper, place the cake on a plate. Powder with icing sugar and serve in small pieces.

Tip! It's a good idea to use a tin with a good coating so that the cake doesn't stick. Nevertheless it can help to cut out a piece of greaseproof paper, brush it with oil and lay it in the bottom of the tin. If you use an ordinary cake tin, it may be best to line both the bottom and the sides with paper.

Nut brittle

Not so healthy and you have to mind your fillings, but now and again you can allow yourself a little treat. And then it's better to make your own so you know what is in it.

250 g mixed nuts
200 g caster sugar

1. Line a baking tray with greaseproof paper. Roast the nuts in a dry frying pan and rub the skin off in a tea towel as much as possible.

2. Melt the sugar slowly in a saucepan until it begins to turn golden brown. Stir in the nuts and bring the nut brittle mix to the boil again.

3. Spread the mixture on the baking tray and leave to cool and set. Break into bite-sized pieces.

WHAT IS ALMOND PASTE?

Almond paste is ground almonds mixed with icing sugar and often also with glucose syrup or egg white to bind it. Almond paste is often made up with apricot or peach kernels in the food industry. Apricots and peaches are related to almonds.

Student toffee

I've seen this sort of bag of sweets all over Europe and it's also called 'student mix' or in German 'Studentfutter' (= 'student tuck'). It provides a lot of nutrition and energy and can be a good thing before an exam or other demanding exercise. But it tastes good any time of course.

1/3 dark chocolate, preferably 70% cocoa content
1/3 mixed nuts
1/3 raisins

Yes, just break the chocolate into small pieces and mix with your favourite nuts and raisins in a bowl or bag.

WHAT IS MARZIPAN?

This is a confectioner's paste which contains more sugar than almonds. Bitter almond oil is often added to provide flavour. The structure of the paste is finer than almond paste and better suited to making shapes. Before the paste can be used different methods are usually used to dry it and cook it to achieve the best consistency.

Almond paste

It's easy and fun to make your own almond paste but you need a good old-fashioned nut grinder I think. Try making the paste with different nuts. Walnut paste is very nice and a paste made of hazelnuts isn't so bad either. The principle is simple, half nuts, half icing sugar and a little egg white to bind the mixture. I don't usually blanch the almonds since I think the flavour is better with the skins on.

400 g almonds or nuts
400 g icing sugar
Egg white

1. Grind the almonds or nuts twice and mix with the icing sugar.

2. Add the egg white, a little at a time, until the paste is just sticky enough and smooth. You won't necessarily need all the white.

Tip! There are icing sugars with all different flavours. Try for instance using chocolate icing sugar with hazelnuts or flavour ordinary icing sugar with 1 tbsp cocoa. Delicious with different cake fillings and sweets coated in chocolate.

Tip! If you use a food processor or blender your mixture will be a little coarser. It doesn't really matter and above all it's quicker if you are in a hurry..

A lot of us undoubtedly think of Lübeck and the skilled confectioners in that city who make marzipan figures in the most fantastic shapes. But anyone who's been to Sicily knows that the Sicilians are at least equally skilled and the island's confectioners vie with one another to make beautiful and delicious creations in marzipan and almond paste. In Italian almond paste is called 'pasta reale', marzipan is quite simply marzipan.

Almond paste log

*A home-made treat which is quick
to make*

200 g almond or other nut paste
(see page 135)
50 g chopped raisins
100 g chopped mixed nuts
Grated rind of 1 organic orange

100 g chocolate

1. Roll out the paste. Sprinkle with raisins,
   nuts and orange peel. Roll up like a Swiss
   roll. Seal the ends and the seam.

2. Lay the log on a piece of greaseproof
   paper. Melt the chocolate over a pan of hot
   water and spread it over the log, it doesn't
   matter if it runs off the sides, and garnish
   with nuts. Allow the chocolate to set and
   cut slices from the log, eat with a cup of
   espresso for example.

The range of pure nut liqueurs available is fairly limited.
The best known is Amaretto which is an Italian almond liqueur.
The flavour comes from a mixture of almonds, apricot kernels
and bitter almond oil.

Sweet drinks with coconut liqueur are usually something we
associate with holidays. Malibu is a coconut liqueur based on rum.
In general you could say that nut liqueurs are best used in drinks
with other, less sweet, ingredients.

Nut liqueurs are of course also
delicious as a flavouring in gateaux,
cakes and desserts.

Often when you are on holiday
you can find nut liqueurs of various
kinds and it's quite a nice souvenir
to bring home. In both Spain and
Italy I have come across different
kinds of almond liqueur. In
Germany I have found hazelnut
liqueur and I have a friend who has
a bottle of cashew wine from the
Philippines at home. It's completely
undrinkable but fun to have as a
keepsake!

Hazelnut espresso

Test your nut liqueur in coffee. In Italy there is a coffee like this called caffe nocciolato.

30 ml espresso
1 tbsp dark muscovado sugar
30 ml hazelnut liqueur or some other nut liqueur
A scoop of whipping cream

Pour the hot coffee into a cup, stir in the sugar and liqueur, top off with a scoop of whipped cream.

A summer drink

40 ml cognac
10 ml nut liqueur
200 ml ice-cold milk
Crushed ice

Nutmeg

Mix together, grate a little nutmeg over and serve with a straw.

Nutritional values nut by nut

PER 100 G NUTS

	cashew nuts	hazelnuts	walnuts	pistachio nuts
kcal	581	644.2	659.6	601.6
protein	15 g	13 g	14.3 g	20.5 g
fat	46 g	62.6 g	62 g	48.5 g
carbohydrates	26 g	9.3 g	13.1 g	22 g
vitamin E	7.4 mg	21 mg	2.6 mg	5.2 mg
calcium	45 mg	188 mg	94 mg	135 mg
iron	6 mg	3.6 mg	2.1 mg	6.7 mg
sodium	16 mg	3 mg	10 mg	6 mg

	brazil nuts	coconut	sweet almonds	peanuts, dried
kcal	657.2	335.3	595.1	570.7
protein	14.3 g	3.4 g	20 g	25.7g
fat	66 g	33.5 g	52 g	49 g
carbohydrates	3.8 g	6.2 g	13.3 g	8.1 g
vitamin E	7.5 mg	3 mg	24 mg	9.1 mg
calcium	176 mg	14 mg	265 mg	58 mg
iron	2.8 mg	1.8 mg	5.2 mg	3.2 mg
sodium	2 mg	20 mg	11 mg	16 mg

	macadamia nuts	pecan nuts	pine nuts
kcal	716	691	673
protein	8 g	9 g	14 g
fat	76 g	72 g	68 g
carbohydrates	13 g	14 g	13 g
vitamin E	–	3.1 mg	0.8 mg
calcium	70 mg	70 mg	16 mg
iron	2.7 mg	2.5 mg	5.5 mg
sodium	4.9 mg	0 mg	2 mg

Index of recipes

Appetisers, accompaniments and starters

Antipasto platter with nuts
Bruschetta with chicken liver paté and walnuts
Chicken liver paté
Grapefruit with tiger prawns and pine nuts
Mussels with curry and pine nuts
Parma ham with cheese and nut cream
Pissaladière with pine nuts and thyme
Pistachio nuts with aniseed
Prawns, garlic and almonds
Salted roasted almonds or nuts
Serrano ham with Manchego cheese and walnuts
Small tortillas with potatoes, leeks and almonds
Spicy almonds
Spicy macadamias

Salads and soups

Ajo blanco
Artichocke salad
Asian soup with noodles and roasted peanuts
Creamy artichoke soup with red caviar and roasted
   hazelnuts
Crisp green salad with hazelnuts
Gado gado salad
Green bean salad with roasted almonds
Prawn soup with roasted almonds
Salad with oyster mushrooms and Brazil nuts, with
   salsa
Savoy cabbage soup with chicken balls and hazelnuts
Waldorf salad

Pasta dishes

Cannelloni with Jerusalem artichokes and
   cashew nuts
Conchiglie with tomato sauce, aubergine and almonds
Pasta with tomato sauce, prawns and pistachio nuts
Pasta sauce with spinach and roasted walnuts
Spaghetti with anchovies and pine nuts

Fish dishes

Fish au gratin with an almond coating
How about zander
Herring fillets with lemon and pine nuts
Oven-baked plaice with red butter
Scampi with pesto gratin

Poultry and other meat

Beef kebabs with peanuts and rice noodles
Burgers with picada, hazelnuts and cheese
Chicken breast with pecan nuts and lemon
   sauce
Chicken casserole with lives and almonds
Chicken kebabs with peanut sauce
Chicken with coconut
Entrecôte with hazelnut butter and spring
   vegetables
Lamb kebabs with pine nuts
Lamb chops with pistachio coating
Minute steaks with spring onions, ginger
   and hazelnuts
Stuffed aubergines
Turkey fillet with walnut and gorgonzola filling

Vegetarian dishes

Baked beetroot with roasted hazelnuts
Broccoli quiche with walnuts
Cauliflower curry with almonds and raisins
Courgette in strips with onion, parmesan and
   pine nuts
Nut cutlets
Parsnip quiche with almonds
Pie pastry
Risotto with onions and Brazil nuts

Sauces, patés and other accompaniments

Almond sauce with a flavour of the Middle East

Aubergine paté with hazelnuts
Avocado and mango paté with cashew nuts
Gremolata with walnuts or pecan nuts
Hazelnut butter
Mayonnaise by hand
Mayonnaise in a mixer or food processor
Pesto alla trapanese
Pesto for an empty purse with treasures from the larder
Pesto genovese
Pesto with hazelnuts
Pesto with pistachio nuts
Pesto with walnuts
Petra's tasty dressing with hazelnuts
Picada
Roasted peppers
Romesco sauce with almonds
Saffron cream with chilli and roasted macadamia nuts
Salbitxada, hot Catalan sauce
Mixed spiced nuts for all kinds of uses
Tapenade with green olives with cashew nuts
Walnut mayonnaise
Warm peanut sauce

Cheese and nuts
Avocado au gratin with nuts and parma ham
Bruschetta with pine nuts
Cheesy nuts
Hazelnut grapes
Hazelnut roulade with mulled pears

Desserts, cakes and gateaux
A great little pudding
Almond macaroons
Apple cake with nuts and lemon
Calvados baked apples in marzipan

Chocolate and pistachio tarte with raspberries and Baileys
Cones with hazelnut ice cream and chocolate toppings
Figs in rum with roasted pecan nuts
Hazelnut butter
Hazelnut meringues
Lemon pannacotta with pistachio nuts
Spice cake with hazelnut butter and saffron cream
Sweet eggy bread with nuts
Tarte with pecan and macadamia nuts
Tasty hazelnut cake
Walnut ice
Walnut ice with black dates
Walnut gateau

Bread, buns and rusks
Almond buns
Focaccia with almonds and cherry tomatoes
Fruit and nut bread
Nut rusks
Pistachio muffins
Walnut bread

Nut and almond sweets
Almond paste
Coconut balls
Almond paste log
Nut brittle
Nut medallions
Panforte with hazelnuts
Peanut bananas
Student toffee

Nuts in drinks
Hazelnut espresso
A summer drink

SOURCES

Bra Böckers Lexikon
Den virtuella floran,
Swedish Natural History Museum, http://linnaeus.nrm.se
Bonniers stora bok om din trädgård by Karin Berglund, Bonnier Alba 1996

The History of Painting by Sister Wendy Beckett
Dictionary of Symbols by Hans Biedermann
The Oxford Companion for Food by Alan Davidson, OUP
Växternas namn by Jens Corneliuson, Wahlström & Widstrand, 1997
www.artcyclopedia.com
Livsmedelsverket (= Food Council) www.slv.se
www.macadamia.se
www.medicallink.se
www.nutritiondata.com
www.pinenut.com
www.shenet.se

ACKNOWLEDGEMENTS

Kerstin Bergfors
Lisbet Ekberg
Maria Karlsson
Martin Pettersson
Daniela Reffo
Gianna Rubega
Mats Sundqvist

Originally published in Sweden by
Bokförlaget Forum, Box 70321, 107 23 Stockholm
www.forum.se

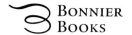

BONNIER
BOOKS

First published in English in 2007
by Bonnier Books
Appledram Barns, Birdham Road
Chichester PO20 7EQ
www.bonnierbooks.co.uk

Published in the English language by arrangement
with Bonnier Group Agency, Stockholm, Sweden

Translated by Julie Martin for First Edition Translations Ltd., Cambridge.

ISBN: 978-1-905825-44-8

Copyright (C) 2005 Maria Fredin Skoog
Concept, text, recipes and test cooking Maria Fredin Skoog
Styling Maria Fredin Skoog and Gunnar Nydrén
Photos Gunnar Nydrén
Photo Ricardo Damiano p. 14 (top)
Printed at Korotan, Ljubljana, Slovenia